# THE WAR OF THE LITTLE ENGLISHMAN

# The War of the Little Englishman

*Enclosure riots on a lonely Welsh hillside*

## EIRIAN JONES

*I'm rhieni, Manod ac Ann*

Thanks to Ann Lenny for the cover image and other photos,
and to Dafydd Prys for the maps. Photo of Hendre, Llan-non
by permission of Llyfrgell Genedlaethol Cymru/the National
Library of Wales. Image of Scremby Hall from the Local Studies
Collection. Lincoln Central Library, by courtesy of Lincolnshire
County Council. Manuscript by permission of the National
Archives at Kew. Thanks to Jeremy Hooker and Stephen Stuart-
Smith for permission to use 'Englishman's Road'.

First impression: 2007
© Eirian Jones and Y Lolfa Cyf., 2007

*This book is subject to copyright and may not be reproduced by
any means except for review purposes without the prior written
consent of the publishers.*

Cover design: Y Lolfa
ISBN: 9 781 84771 0 000
ISBN-10: 184771000 X

Printed on acid-free and partly recycled paper
and published and bound in Wales by
Y Lolfa Cyf., Talybont, Ceredigion SY24 5AP
*e-mail* ylolfa@ylolfa.com
*website* www.ylolfa.com
*tel* 01970 832 304
*fax* 832 782

# INTRODUCTION

THIS BOOK RECOUNTS THE adventures of an English gentleman, who came to a desolate hillside in mid-Wales in the 1820s, to procure a country estate. He had inherited £4,000 from his Lincolnshire-born father but was totally unaware of what might befall him when he spent nearly half of the bequest in buying 856 acres of common land from the government in 1819. A letter written in 1821 to the then Home Secretary sums up his time on the Mynydd Bach to date:

> Since I came into possession I have been the object of unceasing persecution. I began to improve my property by fencing, reducing into cultivation, and building; my fences were thrown down, and in the space of thirteen months, five times successively, have buildings been erected by me and destroyed, in spite of every precaution, by mobs, riotously assembled and in most instances disguised and armed – I have frequently been assaulted with stones; my dwelling has repeatedly been fired with ball.[1]

Brackenbury was not exaggerating and he fails to mention that, one night, he was very nearly roasted alive by the mob, when buttons on his frock coat became too hot to touch, according to local folklore.

Augustus Brackenbury (1792-1874) spent much of the 1820s on Mynydd Bach, a boggy upland area of mid Cardiganshire. He tried to live with the locals and develop a hunting and shooting estate. Finally, in 1829, having evidently endured enough persecution, he decided to sell up and return to England.

This is a story of an Englishman all at sea amongst mainly monolingual, Welsh, hill people, a wealthy man residing in a poor, deprived area, his ambitions being thwarted by the local inhabitants' pure necessity in finding enough food to eat every day. A clash of cultures and a war of words ensued.

## Chapter I

# MYNYDD BACH:
## ITS LOCATION AND BRIEF
## HISTORY

MYNYDD BACH IS A bleak, barren but beautiful place. Solitude can be almost guaranteed amongst its lakes, gorse clad slopes and crumbling stone walls. As a locality, the name Mynydd Bach may not be familiar to many Ceredigion residents, as it is an area of the county, rather than one individual place. In fact, Mynydd Bach seems to be a popular name for upland areas in Wales as there are two areas called Mynydd Bach in Ceredigion and a further one in south Wales, to mention but three.

The Mynydd Bach we have in question here is in the middle of the county of Ceredigion, or Cardiganshire as it was known before the reorganization of the counties of Pembrokeshire, Carmarthenshire and Cardiganshire into the one county of Dyfed in the early 1970s. Mynydd Bach's heart lies around twelve miles south east of the university town and seaside resort of Aberystwyth; seven or eight miles inland from the Georgian, coastal, tourist centre of Aberaeron; six miles to the north west of the famous

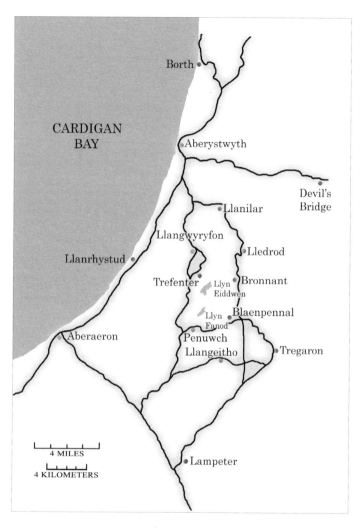

*Map of north Ceredigion*

drovers' town and trekking centre of Tregaron; and a little further to the north east again from the university town of Lampeter.

Mynydd Bach, when translated into English, means little mountain, but it is not a mountain in truth, but a hilly tract, which rises to about a thousand feet at its peak.

The name Mynydd Bach seems only to have been recorded in books and journals since 1813, although there was mention of Llanaeddwen Hills in the Coleman Manuscripts of 1763 (Llyn Eiddwen is the name of one of the area's lakes). However, one local historian, the Rev. D Edwardes, suggested, in his pamphlet entitled *Mynydd Bach* (1914), that the name may have been in use since the sixth century, when the saints Gwynlleu (whose cousin was Saint David) and Gronw lived in the locality, near the site of the present church at Nancwnlle.

The Romans left their mark on the Mynydd Bach, and the remains of a fort can still be seen at nearby Gaerwen. There is also the Sarn Helen road, which runs alongside Mynydd Bach. During Roman times, the local inhabitants would have been members of the Demetae tribe, and it was only after the Romans left that an unit called Ceredigion came into being. By the Middle Ages, Ceredigion was split into divisions of land known as hundreds and commotes, and Mynydd Bach was located in the hundred of Upper Aeron, with the boundaries of the commotes of Anhuniog, Myfenydd and Pennard meeting in the Mynydd Bach area. This system stayed in place until the Act of Union of 1536, after which, Mynydd Bach was placed in the hundred of Ilar.

Mynydd Bach's scattered nature, in geographical terms, has made defining the exact boundaries of the area difficult. Many local observers would include parts of the following villages and hamlets within its fringe: Llangwyryfon, Trefenter, Bronnant, Blaenafon, Blaenpennal and Bethania. In fact, Anne Kelly Knowles, in her book *Calvinists Incorporated* (1997) (which examined the emigration of thousands of Mynydd Bach residents to the United States in the middle of the nineteenth century), suggested the inclusion of the fourteen parishes north of the river Aeron in the Mynydd Bach area, such as Trefilan, Llanddeiniol, Llanychaearn and Lledrod Isaf. She also proposed that it might be land over 800 feet in height which should be regarded as the 'true' Mynydd Bach. Some local residents have another idea however. They are adamant that the name *bwlch*, which means gate, is an important factor. There are many farms and homesteads on Mynydd Bach which incorporate *bwlch* in their name: between Trefenter and Llangwyryfon, there is a farm called Bwlch y Mynydd (gate of the mountain); another similarly named farm is in Bethania; a farm called Bwlch-gwynt (wind, as in weather) in Pen-uwch; a Bwlch Cyrtau in Blaenpennal, and a Bwlchgeuffordd (gate to close the road) in the village of Bronnant. If one were to draw a line linking all these homesteads together, then this would be the true limit of Mynydd Bach, according to local residents.

The Ystwyth fault line runs across Ceredigion from Llanrhystud in the south west to Cwmystwyth in the north east, and therefore cuts through Mynydd Bach. Around fifteen thousand years ago, during the last ice age, the area was covered by the Central Cardiganshire glacier. As the climate warmed, grasses and sedges began to grow and the landscape of the Mynydd Bach would have looked rather similar to the way it does today. Trees such as elm, oak and alder grew too, but it is thought that, during the Bronze Age, many of these trees were felled and the land was developed for agriculture.

The land was poor for farming then, and remains so, even today. The main reason for this is that the soil is peaty in nature and much of the upper reaches of Mynydd Bach are boggy and marshy. However, in the past, this peaty soil has also offered many benefits to the local residents, as up until the 1970s, many of them would gather to cut large blocks of peat out of the ground, usually in the months of April and May. The peat would then be dried over the summer months and would eventually be used to fire the ovens of kitchens in the area throughout the rest of the year. Peat cutting was regarded as an important and valuable local 'right' in the area, and as we shall see later, any threats to this 'right' were regarded with intense disapproval.

Amidst the boggy and marshy upper reaches of Mynydd Bach, two lakes are to be found. Mynydd Bach had three lakes at one time, but the third lake, Llyn Farch (towards the village of Pen-uwch), dried up. Local folklore predicted that once Llyn Farch dried up, then the town of Carmarthen would flood and in time disappear beneath the waves. Llyn Farch has long disappeared, but Carmarthen still thrives.

The other two lakes, Llyn Eiddwen and Llyn Fanod

(the first named after a woman, the second after a man), are natural, reasonably shallow lakes. Llyn Eiddwen lies towards the hamlet of Trefenter, whilst Llyn Fanod is near to Pen–uwch. Both lakes have seen contentious times, and this will be discussed later. A young man called Mark Tredwell also contributed to Llyn Eiddwen's colourful history. In the late nineteenth century, he decided to build a house with a tower on the one acre island located in the middle of Llyn Eiddwen.

Mark Tredwell's father, Solomon, a builder of railway lines in Great Britain and in India, died on the sub-continent when his son was three years old. In 1877, Mark came of age and inherited his father's wealth and, a year later, he made the decision to come to Aberystwyth, to spend his inheritance. He took the lease of a small mansion at Aberllolwyn, Llanfarian, but decided that he also wanted a rural residence, in order to hunt and shoot. He heard about the island in the middle of Llyn Eiddwen and chose to build a house and tower there. Today, the house is a ruin, but it is remembered locally as an example of a folly of the time.

He commissioned the builders Messrs T and W Bubb from Terrace Road, Aberystwyth, to make some improvements to his mansion at Aberllolwyn and to build the house on Llyn Eiddwen. A quarry, which is still known as Tredwell's Quarry, was opened on the Foel, near Llyn Eiddwen, to source stone for the building works. The stone was transported by horse and cart down to the water's edge, before being transferred onto boats and rowed the hundred yards to the island. Wood, slate, sand, lime and workmen were carried in the same way. A wall was built to surround the island. The house included two small rooms and the said tower. It is thought that around a thousand tonnes of stone were used in the construction process.

Tredwell had some other ambitious ideas to offer the places he now called home. For example, he hoped to give a lifeboat and fire engine for service in the town of Aberystwyth. He also created a Volunteer Corps, a small private army, which he dressed in a red uniform; he made them fight mock battles on Mynydd Bach. He apparently kept a yacht called *Baby* on Llyn Eiddwen, and would think nothing of sending a workman some twelve miles to Aberystwyth, to fetch cigars and brandy for his visiting friends from England. Many young ladies were drawn from far a field to visit Tredwell and Mynydd Bach.

These extravagances were costly and led, in part, to his decision to leave Mynydd Bach. When Messrs Bubb had completed the construction of his house on Llyn Eiddwen, they handed him an invoice for £1,319. Tredwell decided to pay £679, as he was of the opinion that Messrs Bubb had overcharged him. The disputants ended up in court and Tredwell was made to pay an additional £538.13.8 to the Bubbs. Tredwell soon tired of Cardiganshire after this episode, and despite spending a great deal of his money, three years later, he moved elsewhere.

The area surrounding Llyn Eiddwen can be described as an unspoilt wilderness. Llyn Eiddwen itself is the source of the river Aeron, which pours into the sea at Aberaeron. Today, the landscape around the lake is dominated by

Molina and purple moor grasses, wild bilberry and acres of Forestry Commission fir trees. There are but a few examples of native trees. Those that do survive are wind-bent, leaning heavily to the north east, as the frequent south westerly winds have left their impression on them.

Today, the red kite flutters elegantly above the moor land. Sheep are dotted all over the hillsides, grazing and occasionally breaking the silence with their bleating. On a clear day, the summit of Mynydd Bach affords excellent views of Pembrokeshire and the Llŷn peninsula. The area

*Llyn Eiddwen today.*

is criss-crossed by C class single track roads and stone walls in need of some maintenance. Isolated farmsteads and ruins fleck the countryside. Amenities are few and far between. Shops and schools have virtually disappeared, as the population of Mynydd Bach in the twentieth century has declined in numbers. There are very few families with young children living there these days. Two village schools, for the children of Blaenpennal and Trefenter, closed in the late 1970s and early 1980s, as a result of the lack of youngsters. Village shops and farmers' markets closed their doors, too, in that period. Chapels have seen a decline in congregations; many have been deconsecrated, with their worshippers merging with other struggling congregations at other chapels. However, a number of unoccupied houses, which fell into ruin in the middle of the last century, have been renovated. This process started in the 1970s, and some of these renovated cottages are now second homes, but most are occupied throughout the year by those who chose to retire to this quiet place. Mynydd Bach certainly did not suffer the wrath of Welsh extremists burning second homes in the 1970s, as happened in other parts of rural Wales.

Mynydd Bach has a rich literary heritage. In the twentieth century, four local sons: E Prosser Rhys, J M Edwards, T Hughes Jones and B T Hopkins, who were all born at about the same time, wrote poetry and prose which won great acclaim nationally. In August 1992, during the National Eisteddfod week in Aberystwyth, a monument was unveiled to these four sons, in appreciation of the great work that they had achieved in Welsh literary life. The monument overlooks Llyn Eiddwen, and a befitting line of *cynghanedd* (special metre) from the hand of E Prosser Rhys is written on it. *Uwch llonyddwch Llyn Eiddwen,* it says, which translates to 'above the quietness of Llyn Eiddwen'.

E Prosser Rhys (1901–1945), who was born in Trefenter, was a remarkable man. Despite suffering from consumption from a young age and missing a great deal of schooling as a result, he became a journalist and, in no time at all, the editor of one of Wales's most popular Welsh weekly newspapers, *Baner ac Amserau Cymru*. He was also a poet and won the Crown prize for a controversial long poem in free metre, at the National Eisteddfod in Pontypool in 1924. He established Gwasg Aberystwyth, a publishing house in Aberystwyth, and published the work of many famous Welsh poets.

J M Edwards (1903–78) was born in Llanrhystud. He spent his life teaching, mostly in Barry, and was a prolific poet, who won the Crown at the National Eisteddfod on three occasions, in the late 1930s and early 1940s. T Hughes Jones (1895–1966) was born in Blaenpennal and, despite writing a good deal of poetry in his youth, it was the novel which became his favourite literary genre, and he published several, including *Amser i Ryfel* (1944), which depicted his experiences during World War II. He later became a lecturer and deputy headmaster, and spent most of his adult life in the Newtown area.

B T Hopkins (1897–1981) was the only one of the four poets to stay on the Mynydd Bach throughout his life. He raised a family and farmed in Blaenpennal. Professor Gwyn

Williams, who retired to the Mynydd Bach after years of teaching at universities in Turkey, Libya and Egypt, claims that B T Hopkins's *cywydd* (a poem written in *cynghanedd*) to *Rhos Helyg* is the best thing ever written about the Mynydd Bach. It certainly made him well-known in literary circles in Wales.

Yet another prolific writer, J Myfenydd Morgan, who

*Monument to four local poets: E. Prosser Rhys, J. M. Edwards, T. Hughes Jones and B. T. Hopkins, which overlooks Llyn Eiddwen.*

was brought up in the area at the end of the nineteenth century, called the inhabitants of Mynydd Bach the *pobl y pennau hirion*, which translates to 'people with long heads', meaning people with high intellect. Indeed, this remote place seems to have produced very many men of letters.

★   ★   ★

This book seeks to examine the events which occurred on the Mynydd Bach in Augustus Brackenbury's day, a period of ten years, up to the year 1829. Brackenbury, an English country gentleman from the county of Lincolnshire, arrives on Mynydd Bach in 1819, but what kind of place does he encounter?

Brackenbury arrived at a time when the population of Mynydd Bach was on the rise. Census returns collected from 1801 show that the total population of all thirteen parishes of Mynydd Bach was 6,237. By 1821, the population had grown by nearly a third, to 8,138, and, twenty years later, a population of 9,133 was recorded for 1841. But, by 1851, a decline had set in, and the reasons for that will be outlined later.

A number of explanations have been offered for the large increase in population in the early decades of the 1800s. At this time, there was a significant improvement in the general standard of living throughout the area. Land was becoming more readily available, due to the implementation of the enclosure acts, and, as a result, more food was being produced. Some advances were being made in house building too, and houses in general were of better quality. As a result, infant mortality began to fall and older people began to live longer. With a healthier population than previously and the number of inhabitants increasing, there was bound to be increased pressure on land. There was very little low lying land which hadn't already been enclosed and occupied. Therefore, as soon as all the fertile land on the lower slopes of the hills had been taken, inhabitants looked further up the hills (where conditions were not as favourable), for a few fields to cultivate. Many people turned their sights to farming Mynydd Bach land, as this was the only available land left.

These new prospectors changed the landscape of Mynydd Bach for ever. Many of them were itinerant people, who would work occasionally, helping to gather in the harvests on tenant farms. They probably owned a cow or two, a few sheep and some geese, which would graze on the common land. All these new farmers, or squatters, as many of the locals called them, had to live somewhere. This need for local housing led to the illegal, but within local tradition acceptable, phenomenon known as building a *tŷ unnos*, not only on the hills of Mynydd Bach, but on hills all over Wales. *Tŷ unnos* translates as one night house, which is the length of time it took to build one.

A *tŷ unnos* had to be built on land which was relatively dry throughout the year as the floor of the house would be left as bare earth. It was also important for the house to be located near a source of water, such as Llyn Eiddwen, for example, on Mynydd Bach. At sunset, a man would go to the desired location of his prospective new home. Prior to this, he would have prepared a door, a frame for a window and trusses for the roof of the new house. He would then, in the gathering gloom, set about building the walls of his house with turf. Once this was done, crossbeams for the roof would be placed on top of the walls. Rushes and sticks, which would have been gathered previously, would later be placed on the roof itself. He would also ensure that a hole was left in the roof, so that smoke from the fire could escape. The final objective, before daybreak, was to light a fire inside the new house. Building these houses in such a short space of time was an amazing feat, especially considering that, unless one happened to be fortunate and built it on a moonlit night, all this construction work had to be done in pitch darkness.

Once the house was erected, it was then decided how much land should be allocated to the new house. Tradition had it that the new owner would stand at his front door and throw an axe as far as he could. The spot where the axe fell determined the boundary of his home. From this point, a semicircle was drawn back towards the house, and this would be its enclosed land. Further to this, it was necessary that someone was at home constantly, for the period of a whole year and a day. According to local custom, if the house was left empty at any point within that time span, a total stranger could enter and claim ownership of the house. As soon as the builder had been in residence for a year and a day, stone and soil mortar were used to build more permanent walls on the outside of the house, and once this was done, the original house was dismantled from within and taken out through the front door. Building these houses was a tradition and a way of

*A local example of a* tŷ *unnos: Hendre, Llan-non, Ceredigion.*

life in these parts. *Tai unnos* certainly weren't legally the property of the owners, and the land enclosed around the new house was still common land, as such, but there were exceptions, as will be outlined in the following chapter.

Most houses on the upper reaches of Mynydd Bach were of this type, in the early 1800s. Often the houses were divided into two rooms, with one room for the people to occupy and the other for the family's animals, such as a cow or a pig. Some of the better houses in the area had slate roofs. These were regarded locally as being mini palaces. If money were available in later years, the owner would possibly build a third house on the site, constructed of quarried stone with sand mortar and lime. This house would have larger windows and, perhaps, two floors. It is surprising how many of these houses are still standing on Mynydd Bach today.

According to the census returns of the early 1800s, nearly sixty percent of men on Mynydd Bach earned their living from agriculture, in some form or other. About fifteen per cent would have been craftsmen, such as butchers, carpenters, millers or stone masons, with another one in ten involved in drapery, visiting homesteads, to collect orders from the occupants, who wanted clothes. Sixty per cent of women who were in paid work were maids or servants, whilst another one in ten worked as labourers.

What was life like for these people on this isolated hillside in the early decades of the nineteenth century? Let's take the example of a family man, who toiled the land and lived in one of these typical one night houses. Whilst the husband would be cutting peat or tending to his animals during the day, his wife would be busy in the home, making butter and cheese from the milk of the family cow. She probably kept a few hens and geese, and any surplus eggs would be passed on to traders, and sold later in the markets of towns such as Llanelli, Merthyr Tudful and Hereford. The family might own a pig and, having fattened it over the summer, it would be slaughtered for meat to eat during the leaner winter months.

In the evenings, the farmer's wife would knit socks, primarily for the family but also to sell in the local markets. However, there wouldn't be a great need for socks in the summer time, when everyone went around in bare feet at that time, with the exception of the excursion to chapel on a Sunday, when clogs would be worn, out of respect. Clothes would be made in the home, from the wool off the backs of the roaming sheep. The wool would be spun, and then woven into cloth, with a local draper coming to the home to make some garments out of the same cloth for every member of the household.

Schooling for the Mynydd Bach children was infrequent, at best. There was a school a good three to four mile walk away, but this was only held for three or four months in the winter time. Many children, even the youngest, would have jobs to do around the home and in the fields, which would reduce the amount of time given to education. When at school, these monolingual Welsh children (normally taught by male teachers who weren't Welsh linguists) would try to learn to read English, do some writing, and learn Latin and some mathematics. It was forbidden to speak Welsh in these schools, and the system of Welsh Not was in operation. A Welsh Not was a piece of wood, about an inch and a half long and half an inch wide, with the letters W and N carved onto it. Any child heard speaking a word of Welsh would be handed the Welsh Not, and woe betide the child who ended up with this particular piece of wood, at the end of the school day. He or she would be in for quite a lashing from the teacher. However, from the age of ten onwards, children wouldn't receive any more schooling whatsoever, as at about that age, they were expected to go out and earn a living as farm hands or a maids on neighbouring farms.

On a Sunday, attending chapel was particularly important. Mynydd Bach was a very religious area at the beginning of the nineteenth century. Augustus Brackenbury himself came from a family with strong Wesleyan Methodist connections, and many of his brothers and cousins became Church of England clergymen. Probably unbeknown to Augustus on his arrival in Cardiganshire, he had purchased land not many miles from the cradle of the Welsh Calvinistic Methodist tradition.

Around a century prior to Augustus Brackenbury's arrival on Mynydd Bach, Daniel Rowland, the vicar of the parish of Llangeitho, a village about five or six miles from Mynydd Bach, was converted to Methodism, after listening to the sermon of Griffith Jones, a famous Welshman, who founded many schools for the poor all over Wales, in the eighteenth century. As a result of Rowland's conversion and his questioning of what the state Church was offering to its parishioners, Llangeitho became the focus of feverish evangelical activity, with Daniel Rowland's sermons attracting thousands of pilgrims each Sunday, from all over Wales. Even after his death in 1790, many of the faithful from Mynydd Bach would prefer to travel to Llangeitho and take communion in Daniel Rowland's chapel. By 1811, the Methodists formally separated from the state Church, and this led to another revival in faith in 1812 and the building of Methodist Chapels in several locations on Mynydd Bach. A *second* chapel was built in Blaenpennal in 1812.

Later on in the nineteenth century, open air prayer meetings, called *Cwrdd Gweddi'r Mynydd,* were held on Mynydd Bach. In its heyday, at the beginning of the twentieth century, thousands of worshippers would attend for two or three days, at the end of June, to pray, sing hymns and listen to sermons in the open air. They wouldn't necessarily be locals either, as people from all over Wales made the journey. Such prayer meetings are still held today, but on a much smaller scale; one such is now held indoors, at Bethel chapel, in Trefenter, on a Sunday at the end of June, and these days, one service is held, instead of the three day event of a century earlier. Mynydd Bach maintained a strong Methodist tradition throughout the last century, and this has only begun to wane in recent times.

Attending chapel on a Sunday, in the early 1800s, was deemed of great importance, not only as a means of one showing ones faith, but also as a focal point for meeting others who lived on more isolated parts of the hills. Mynydd Bach residents socialized in other ways too. Farmers' markets would be held regularly, and the market held at Pen-uwch was probably the nearest for the residents of Mynydd Bach, at a good hour's walk away. This market was important predominantly for the sale of cattle and apples. In another direction, towards the town of Aberystwyth, lay Lledrod market, and here cattle and horses were peddled. In Llangeitho, there was another fair, at which cattle were sold, but this one was also a hiring fair, where servants could find new masters and mistresses, and vice versa. Markets were a place to buy and sell and also places to visit to have a good time and forget the hardships of life for a few hours. The cheap cider would often be consumed to extremes, and this would lead to many an alcohol-induced fight. Those not inclined to drink their woes away could content themselves by listening to the balladeer telling the latest news of events from around the country, such as murders and shipwrecks.

Despite the occasional merriment, life in the first two

decades of the nineteenth century was very difficult for the hill farmers of Mynydd Bach. The Napoleonic Wars had come to an end in 1815, and although those events took place a great distance away from the rural inhabitants of Mynydd Bach, the effect of those wars certainly had an impact on them. During the wars, there had been inflationary pressures on the economy, and the fighting had obscured this from people's thoughts. The first signs of impending trouble arrived in 1813. There was an excellent harvest that year and, as a result of the surpluses, the prices of commodities such as wheat and barley fell. With the end of the war, in 1815, the returning soldiers caused more unemployment, which added to the pressures on the economy. The wars had also created a huge national debt. In order to keep up the price of corn (a vital commodity in the economy of the day), the Corn Laws were passed in 1815, but the situation still deteriorated. Only small quantities of stock and corn were sold, at very low prices, in the Cardiganshire markets and fairs. In addition, Cardiganshire suffered awful weather in 1816, and, as a result, a famine was widespread in the county in 1817.

The small hill farmers of Mynydd Bach suffered terribly. Rents were reduced by the landlords, but it was still a struggle to pay. Money was very scarce and local banks collapsed or stopped payment. Those people who had borrowed money in the years of inflation were now unable to fulfil their obligations. Sales of properties by farmers facing debt were frequent. Some even entered gaol, and others left Mynydd Bach for good and found a new life in the United States.

Agricultural labourers also felt the pressures of the times. Although their wages did not fall as much as the price of foodstuffs, the peasantry found it far harder to find employment and thus obtain the money to buy the cheap bread. Some of the poor were so desperate for food to eat that they would try to stave off hunger by swallowing barley meal and water, and also by boiling nettles. Many went without food for days on end.

New paupers crowded on to the lists of those in receipt of parish relief, and vagrancy increased. By February 1817, many people went around the Cardiganshire countryside, begging for food and work at the houses of the gentry. The London Association for the Relief of the Manufacturing and Labouring Poor sent money, clothing and food to help those who were starving. A local branch of the Association was formed in the county, but it seems to have collapsed due to lack of support. By 1819, Cardiganshire was spending twice as much on the poor as it had done three years previously.

The poor may have been suffering greatly, but the local gentry had plenty in reserve, to see them through the lean times. Augustus Brackenbury wasn't the only gentleman of fortune living in the Mynydd Bach area. A well established family were the Lloyds who lived at Mabws, Llanrhystud, a couple of miles towards the coast from Mynydd Bach. During the time of John and James Lloyd, in the eighteenth century, the Mabws estate consisted of forty-seven farms in the Llanrhystud area alone, and its estate spread over many square miles of central Cardiganshire. However, the gentlemen of Mabws weren't entirely detached from the suffering of the poor around them in the 1820s. As we shall see in the following chapter, many squires were subjected to a great deal of unsavoury attention, and most of this was due to the enclosure of land.

★ ★ ★

The early decades of the nineteenth century saw a steady increase in the population of Mynydd Bach. However, by the 1841 census, records show that unenclosed land was becoming scarcer and many young families started looking elsewhere to live. The expanding industrial areas of south Wales, and Merthyr Tudful in particular, drew the attention of those seeking a new life and hoping to get out of the cycle of poverty that inflicted them on Mynydd Bach. Other people started to look further afield, and many were attracted to the lights of London, where they hoped to make their fortunes. As they had experience of milking dairy cows, several decided to establish businesses producing and selling milk to the inhabitants of the growing city. Many of the very religious Mynydd Bach residents, however, were concerned with the less savoury influences and the lack of religious propriety of the larger towns and cities, such as Merthyr Tudful and London, and therefore sought other localities in which to reside.

In the 1830s, Edward Jones, a Methodist preacher, took a group of thirty Aberystwyth residents to the United States. This embryonic voyage started a trend of emigration which lasted ten years, culminating in the establishment of a 'little Cardiganshire' in the Jackson and Gallia districts of the State of Ohio. In the following years, up to 1860, 968 Welsh people emigrated to these districts of Ohio; 846, or 87% of them, came from the parishes of Mynydd Bach. This is a quite staggering amount from one small area; indeed, it represents about 15% of the total population of Mynydd Bach seeking to migrate overseas.

Emigration was a costly business and, from 1818, it was only the more prosperous Mynydd Bach residents who could fund their move to the United States. Encouraged by their apparent success in Ohio, it was the turn of tenants who had substantial farms (in Mynydd Bach terms) next, and they emigrated between 1837 and 1841. In the years 1845-7, many people barely on the margins of survival sailed out of Aberystwyth westwards; some were given parish assistance to make the journey. However, by 1850, it seems that the migration from Mynydd Bach was over. With such large numbers departing for London and the United States, there was more land now available on Mynydd Bach for those who had stayed behind.

Augustus Brackenbury came upon Mynydd Bach in 1819. He found an isolated area, where the inhabitants encountered great difficulties simply in surviving from day to day. It is said that it was whilst he was on a touring holiday of Wales that his attention was drawn to Cardiganshire, and Mynydd Bach in particular. An enclosure act, passed into law in 1815, made him decide that his future lay on this bleak and barren Welsh hillside. We will now look further at the Enclosure Acts of the early nineteenth century and assess their implications on the countryside of Cardiganshire.

## Chapter 2

# THE ENCLOSURE OF COMMONS
# IN CARDIGANSHIRE

IT WAS THE PRIVATE Enclosure Act of Llanrhystud Myfenydd, passed on 2 May 1815, in the 55th year of the reign of George III, which brought a naïve, unsuspicious but ambitious Augustus Brackenbury to Mynydd Bach, Cardiganshire, at the tail end of 1819.

This act meant that five thousand acres of common land were put up for sale in the following eight parishes of Mynydd Bach: Gwnnws, Lledrod, Llangriython (Llangwyryfon), Llanilar, Rhostie, Llandinol (Llanddeiniol), Llanych'aiarn (Llanychaearn) and Llanrhystud. Brackenbury bought less than a fifth of this land (856 acres in total), in seven lots, for the sum of £1,750.

The population of Great Britain had been increasing steadily throughout the eighteenth century, and new ways of providing food for its citizens had to be found. In January 1795, a report was commissioned by the British government's recently established Board of Agriculture. This body estimated that, at the time, there were 206,720 acres of Cardiganshire land lying unenclosed, as common fields or waste lands. This meant that the land was not

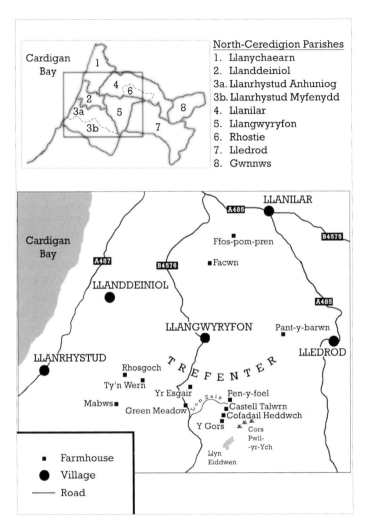

*Map of parishes and homesteads on Mynydd Bach*

being farmed or cultivated by any one individual. It also meant that this land was officially owned by the Crown or government, and that it could be used by everybody who so wished to do so, as common grazing land. If one considers that the acreage of Cardiganshire was 435,492 at the time, one realises that nearly half of the whole county's land, and therefore a substantial amount of land, was in general ownership. No one person had the legal right to develop this land and subsequently improve it with a view to producing more food. Interestingly, some fifty years later (1843), the Tithe Commission estimated that the acreage of unenclosed common and waste lands in Cardiganshire had fallen to 94,910 acres. This shows the impact that the Enclosure Acts had upon the Cardiganshire countryside.

These waste and common lands were highly valued by landowners and owner occupiers alike because they enjoyed certain rights to it. There was the 'right of common', 'the right of pasturage' for horses, sheep and cattle, and the 'right of sheep-walk'. In addition, many of the commons and waste lands supplied fuel in the form of peat, turf and faggots to any person who wanted it. The commons also provided land, although illegally, for squatters to build houses on, as we've seen from the previous chapter's description of *tŷ unnos*. Therefore, the value of this unenclosed land to the inhabitants who lived in its vicinity, rich or poor, cannot be exaggerated. It certainly wasn't the 'waste land' or land of no use to any one that the name suggests. In fact, it was once said that the sheep-walk common land on the mountains attached to a farm, was more valuable than the actual farm itself.

At the turn of the nineteenth century, many of the commons and wasted lands were supervised by the Lord of the Manor and the manor courts. These courts laid down laws concerning what the residents of the area could and could not do on this land. For example, tenants had to make sure that they maintained the fences and gates regularly. If any strangers were found cutting turf on the common, they would be fined 5 shillings for each cartload taken away. However, despite all these rules and laws to maintain order and fairness under the supervision of the manor courts, increasing numbers of squatters encroached on the common, especially towards the end of the eighteenth century and beginning of the nineteenth century. As a result, the acreage of common and waste land managed effectively by the manor courts was reduced considerably. Manor courts seemed to be unable to do much about the encroachment situation. As the nineteenth century dawned, the courts tried to levy a rent on these new 'owner occupiers'. As has already been outlined in Chapter 1, there was a great deal of pressure on the land at this time, due to the increasing population. Encroachment and the Enclosure Acts heightened the tension felt by those inhabitants trying to eke out a living.

Encroachment was sometimes justified because the boundaries of these common and waste lands were often undefined, and this led to confusion and subsequent disorder. For example, on Mynydd Bach, the parishioners of Llanrhystud held a meeting on 4 July 1815, to ask for a decision on the actual boundary between the two lordships of Llanrhystud Myfeneydd and Llanrhystud

Anhuniog. The boundaries of the local gentry's estates were also unmarked, which led to the encroachment of their land too. The estate of Lord Lisburn, at Crosswood, on the edge of Mynydd Bach, had been, according to his lordship's agent, 'enclosed and colonized by the very scum of the earth', and they were costing the estate the sum of £200 per annum. However, the gentry were advised not to proceed against the squatters nor remove them from their land. Past experiences had shown how violent and strong a force the squatters could be, when threatened. Instead, Lord Lisburn tried to raise money in rent from the encroachers, which resulted in the encroachers gaining too. They earned the protection that went hand-in-hand with being the subject of the landlord. But encroachments on the common and private land were multiplying rapidly and a solution was needed to keep both sides content.

Enclosing a piece of land meant surrounding it with fencing and then preparing the land for agricultural practices. As the land would be fenced in, it would then have an individual owner, who was responsible for its upkeep and development. Enclosing land had begun in the reign of Queen Anne, and between 1760 and 1845 nearly four thousand private Acts of Enclosure were placed on the government statute book in Great Britain. These private acts were normally sponsored by local landowners and stipulated that a sufficient majority of the local people had to agree to the enclosure. It is doubtful, however, whether everyone in the area would have had a say in the matter.

The General Enclosure Act of 1801 was designed to make the procedure more cost effective and to ensure that it was easier for the promoter of the legislation to overcome initial hurdles. However, little of the Act's provisions protected the poor parishioners, who would see the common land that they used on a daily basis for grazing taken away from them with little or no recompense. The Act ensured that commissioners were appointed to oversee the needs of local communities. In many cases, however, the role of the commissioners was a particularly challenging one and often the locals found it difficult to find common ground with them and make progress on areas of dispute.

Among the many obstacles to parliamentary enclosure, perhaps the most serious hurdle was that of expense. *The Cambrian* newspaper in 1810 declared that enclosing a common of 2,000 acres could cost up to £1,400 with, for example, the two commissioners employed to oversee the enclosure costing £350, the construction of two miles of public road accounting for another £200, and fees paid for the Bill in the House of Commons requiring a further outlay of £95.

However, these expenses did not dampen the enthusiasm of many landowners for promoting the enclosure of land in their locality. Landowners in the manor of Myfenydd (where Brackenbury bought his land) first showed interest in enclosing land in 1814, but in the neighbouring manor of Llanrhystud Anhuniog, a petition was presented to Parliament on 29 January 1811. However, despite the provisions of the General Enclosure Act of 1801, it was still a rather slow, laborious process. Yet another petition of landowners in the manor of Llanrhystud Anhuniog was needed in 1812, and the Act received royal assent that year.

Charles Hassals and David Joel Jenkins from Lampeter were appointed commissioners to carry out the details of the Act. Hassals died soon after, in 1814, and his place was taken by John Cheese of Lyon's Hall, Hereford. The surveyor for this Act was a John Hughes of Aberystwyth.

Under the terms of the Llanrhystud Anhuniog Act, squatters who'd been in residence (that is, had built a house and enclosed some land around it) for twenty years or more, were allowed to keep their encroachment. How squatters were able to prove to the authorities the length of time they'd been in residence we do not know. It seems most unlikely that the squatter would have had any paper work reflecting the age of his home. However, those who had been in occupancy for less than twenty years lost out dramatically. They had their land referred to as waste and common land, but they were given the opportunity to buy their encroachment back. However, the cost of buying the encroachment did not take into account the buildings that may have been erected on the site. No pecuniary advantage was offered to these squatters for all their hard work.

Another part of the enclosure was set aside by the commissioners, to ensure a sufficient supply of peat for the owners and their tenants within the lordship. Any persons having a surplus of peat were allowed to sell some to the overseers of the poor and any parishes within that lordship, for the use of the paupers. The Enclosure Act of Llanrhystud Anhuniog had to be completed within the stipulated timescale of four years, and in April 1816, all rights of the common came to an end in Anhuniog.

Landowners in the neighbouring manor of Llanrhystud

Myfenydd began to show interest in enclosing their land in 1814. As noted before, this Enclosure Act was passed on 2 May 1815 and would, in time, attract the interest of Augustus Brackenbury to Cardiganshire. This Act was very similar to the previous Llanrhystud Anhuniog Act passed in 1812, but the squatters were treated more generously on this occasion. This, however, did not prevent problems arising and, by 1817, the legality of the right of commons was contested with the commissioner of enclosures. This Act wasn't completed within the stipulated four years either. (Debates concerning the validity of the Act continued until 1835.)

Was enclosing land on Mynydd Bach worthwhile to everyone concerned? It does not seem to have been the case. In the examples of Llanrhystud Anhuniog and Llanrhystud Myfenydd, it was those men who suggested and promoted the Acts in the first instance who had the most to gain: people like the Earl of Lisburn, John Lloyd of Mabws and the Reverend Alban Thomas Jones Gwynne JP: gentlemen who already owned a considerable amount of land and had the financial means to acquire more.

The gentry's motives for enclosing land were genuine, on the whole, as they were eager for the Acts to bring about general agricultural improvement in the area. Agricultural improvement did not necessarily mean just improving the quality of the tilled earth. Fencing or building stone hedges was also considered to be an improvement of the landscape. Another strong motive for enclosure by the landowners was the settling of the encroachment issue, a problem which preyed on their minds a great deal. Many landowners saw a financial gain as well. They were well aware that enclosed land yielded much higher rents than open-field land.

The landowners may have benefited, but the tenant farmers and cottager squatters suffered as a result of the loss of rights of common. Frankland Thomas Lewis, in a report from the Select Committee on Commons Enclosure, described the latter in terms of:

> There is no comparison whatever between the moral state of persons who gain their livelihood by day-labour and those who occupy a cottage and garden, and perhaps a small encroachment in the neighbourhood of a common, and who live as cottiers, not as labourers; they get their livelihood merely from the depasture of the common, or as they can be, by shifting means in their power; they are never so well off; and never educate their children so well; they are much more frequently brought before the magistrates for acts of violence and turbulence than the steady regular day-labourer.[2]

As already noted, the squatters who had built their house and enclosed their land in the last twenty years faced losing their land and home as a result of the Enclosure Acts. This inevitably led to a great deal of resentment and violence. Their land would be sold at public auction, with the purchaser, be it the incumbent or a new owner, being required: 'to pay a deposit of one tenth part of the purchase money at the time of such sale' and to 'give security for the remainder within two calendar months after the said sale, and in default thereof money so deposited will be forfeited'. Very few squatters had the financial means, especially in the dire times of the 1810s, to purchase their encroachments, and this doubtless strengthened their spirit of resistance to the enclosures, as the following example shows.

On or about the 29th of May 1815, John Hughes, the surveyor responsible for drawing up the Anhuniog award, and William Hughes, who was probably a small farmer, visited Mynydd Bach in the line of their duties and were met by a mob of some one hundred and fifty angry people. The mob took John Hughes's measuring chain and theodolite (a surveying instrument for measuring angles), and knocked him flat to the ground. Horns were sounded, and more people appeared on the hillside. The surveyor was warned that, if he returned to Mynydd Bach, he would be murdered. The mob also declared that, if the enclosure commissioners, David Joel Jenkins and John Cheese, tried to execute the Act, they would be buried alive.

In the following months, similar scenes of discontent were enacted. On July 11, when the enclosure commissioners, the surveyor and Evan Evans, the High Constable of the lower division of the hundred of Ilar (where the Mynydd Bach area lay), tried to measure the land, their appearance on the hillside brought out hundreds of incensed men, women and children. John Hughes was threatened again, and Evan Evans was told that, if he repeated his visits with the surveyor, he had better bring a bag with him, in order to carry his bones home.

The rioters were particularly hostile towards the local landowner, John Lloyd of Mabws. He benefited as much as anyone from the enclosure acts (he received some 367 acres of allotments and bought over 46 acres of encroachments and 4 acres of common or waste ground), and was attacked by a large mob of men, women and children. For their part in these disturbances, three labourers from the parish, William James, John Thomas and John Davies, were committed to the county gaol.

John Lloyd received an anonymous letter, warning him that any further attempt at an 'invasion' would be followed by the destruction of not only John Lloyd of Mabws himself, but his family and friends also. As tensions mounted, the peasantry had no qualms in attacking the commissioners, by throwing stones at them. In July 1815, a mob comprised solely of women armed with dripping pans, came down upon John Hughes, the surveyor and his helpers 'like a rolling torrent...' They directed his attention to a pit to be used for the internment of every surveyor who approached their 'rights', as the following letter written by John Lewis implies:

> A dreadful insurrection has broke out in the Mountains surrounding Llanrhystud in consequence of the attempt made by the Commissioners to enclose the common. John Hughes unexpectedly, was surrounded by 30 Old Women, each bearing in point of ferocity an amiable resemblance to the Delphic Sibyl of old. They came down upon him in half Squadrons, *well equipped*, strongly organised, and defended as to the breast by a dripping pan, which acted as a cuirass, and armed with missile weapons of all descriptions. The body was so compact and so united, could not be resisted, his surrender was discreet, his Gaging apparatus was seized

and his attention finally directed to a pit which was dug for the internment of every Surveyor that approached their rights. For some time the very name of an old woman, associated with a mountain or a dripping pan recalled so many frightful images to his recollection, that he felt but little inclined again to attack their territory. But at length reinforced by his Measuring Brethren preceded by some vedetes [scouts] each determined to present a token of remembrance, as a testimony of their regard for the *civility* offered to their Brother; they ascended the hill without interruption, but no sooner had approached the fastnesses, than like a rolling torrent the Amazons rushed down, drove in their vedetes, broke the line and the air resounded with "*Sauve qui peut*" of the dismayed; and the triumphant yell of the Sibyls. A consultation has taken place among the magistrates, a deposition has been sent to Mr Johns, and a troop of horse will be immediately sent to disperse this infuriated mob. *Honestly* speaking this is all true. A letter was sent to Mabus, unsigned, to inform the Colonel that any further attempts at invasion, would be attended with destruction to himself, family and friends. The force is now increased to 200, half of which are Men — all entrenched at an agreeable distance from Mabus.[3]

As a result of these increasing skirmishes, troops were stationed in Aberystwyth, 'to preserve the peace and to aid the civil power in dispersing the tumultuous assemblies of peasantry on the neighbouring hills, who were preventing the Commissioners under a certain Enclosure Act called "The Haminog [Anhuniog] Act" from carrying their measures into execution'. A correspondent of the *Cambrian* newspaper of 24 February 1816 expressed his sense of alarm at the state of affairs, not only on Mynydd Bach, but in several districts of Cardiganshire:

> We regret to hear that several districts in Cardiganshire are very disturbed, and that the Sheriff's officers are incapable of executing their duties. We trust, however, that the prompt and determined manner in which J. H. Williams Esq., the High Sheriff, called in the aid of the Posse Comitatus and a detachment of the Carmarthen Militia, now at Aberystwyth, has convinced the poor deluded rioters that opposition to these laws will be fruitless. Two or three of the ringleaders have been apprehended, and, we are glad to add, without an effusion of blood.

In time, the disturbances abated and peace returned to the hillsides once more. By February 1816, the Mynydd Bach riots were over for the time being and the militia was temporarily disbanded.

The Llanrhystud Anhuniog and Myfenydd Enclosure Acts had created a great deal of mistrust and conflict long before Augustus Brackenbury appeared on the scene in 1819. Opportunistically, he saw a great deal of land being sold off at the reasonable price of a touch over £2 an acre. Despite the poor quality of this land, Augustus Brackenbury seems to have been unfazed by the problems associated with improving it. He also seems to have been totally unaware of the 'troubles' regarding past enclosures of land on Mynydd Bach. But before he sets foot on Mynydd Bach, we need to explore where Augustus Brackenbury came from and what his background could tell us about him.

## Chapter 3

# THE BRACKENBURY FAMILY
# OF LINCOLNSHIRE

THE BRACKENBURYS OF LINCOLNSHIRE were well respected and held prominent positions as lawyers, land owners and clergymen to the inhabitants of this large eastern county. The *Dictionary of National Biography*, mentions four famous Lincolnshire Brackenburys: three are soldiers, Sir Edward of Skendleby, Sir Henry and his brother Charles Booth Brackenbury, and a clergyman and poet named Joseph Brackenbury. However, the dictionary fails to mention Robert Carr Brackenbury, a leading Methodist and a great friend of John Wesley, who was regarded by many as probably the most distinguished member of the whole Brackenbury family. He was also a first cousin of Charles Brackenbury, Augustus's father.

The Brackenbury family took their name from the village of Brackenborough, which is situated about two and a half miles to the north of Louth. Brackenborough is mentioned in *The Domesday Book*. However, the branch of the Brackenbury family tree that holds our attention come from Scremby, further to the south west. It was at Scremby Hall that Augustus Brackenbury was born, on the 17th of February 1792.

Scremby Hall was one of the grander country houses of an area of Lincolnshire known as Spilsbyshire. Scremby Hall was built during the seventeenth century, and in the 1670s, a Charles Newcomen resided there. Thomas Newcomen, of the same family, invented the first coal-powered steam engine to pump water, in 1712. This engine and its subsequent improvements would be used by British and American salt makers. The Moody family took up residence at Scremby Hall at the turn of the eighteenth century. John Moody, who died childless in 1747, bequeathed the Scremby property to his niece Elizabeth Ostler, who married Thomas Carr Brackenbury, Augustus's grandfather.

J C Nattes produced a drawing of Scremby Hall for Sir Joseph Banks, early in the nineteenth century. The illustration shows a three storey house with a central section that was believed to have been built or added to at around 1720. Two side wings with canted bays had been added to the main house by 1800. The brickwork of the central section was of Old English Bond, with the two wings of the house being Flemish Bond brick. Scremby Hall consisted of nine bedrooms and an upstairs library, with the ground floor comprising two dining rooms and drawing rooms (in plans of the building seen from 1937). Scremby boasted beautiful gardens and a large ornamental pond, well stocked with fish. The gardens lay in a glorious wooded park. The house remained in the Brackenbury family until the early twentieth century. As a family home and a place for entertaining other minor gentry families,

*Scremby Hall.*

its heyday, however, had long passed. The house was last occupied in 1937, after which it deteriorated quickly. By 1958, Scremby Hall was being used as a grain store; it was finally demolished in the 1970s, and there are now cattle sheds on the site.

Augustus Brackenbury's family tree reveals a number of generations of Brackenburys. Augustus Brackenbury was descended on his father's side from Miles Brackenbury, a husbandman who died in 1610. His son, who was also named Miles, was a miller, and his son, another Miles, a yeoman, who died in 1645 at Baumber. Miles of Baumber was married to Hester and they had four children. He owned freehold land in Orby, and left £40 to pay for the education of his two elder sons, and £60 to both of his younger children, when they came of age.

One of his sons, Thomas Brackenbury (1637-1702), was Augustus's great, great grandfather and he resided at Great Steeping. He became an attorney. With his first wife, Ann, he had four sons and a daughter. Thomas later married Elizabeth Boddington, a widow. Elizabeth Boddington came from a rich London merchant family, which had trading links with the East Indies. Thomas and Elizabeth produced a further son and three daughters.

Augustus was descended from Carr Brackenbury (1688-1741), son of Thomas and Elizabeth. His first wife, Ann, was the daughter of Langley Gace, a gentleman of Panton and Hardwicke. She died in 1729, and three years after her death, Carr Brackenbury remarried. His second wife, who was also called Ann, was the daughter of another wealthy family; her father, Sir John Tyrwhitt, was the baronet of Stainfield. However, at the time of their marriage, Ann Tyrwhitt was in a considerable amount of debt and Carr had to spend £200, to satisfy many of her creditors. It seems that her father, the baronet, had very little money. Even at the time of Carr's death, some eleven years after their marriage, Sir John Tyrwhitt had still not paid the marriage portion of the £6,000. Carr Brackenbury had planned to use this £6,000 to discharge the mortgage owed to the Trustees of the Duke of Ancaster on one of his properties at Lusby.

Carr Brackenbury and Ann Tyrwhitt produced four children, but only one survived, a son called James. It seems that the wider Brackenbury family did not take too kindly to Ann Tyrwhitt. In her will, she claims 'and whereas the family of the Brackenbury's have not thought it worth their while to pay me any friendly attention'. It is possible that the Brackenburys thought that Ann Tyrwhitt had benefited greatly, in the days when her husband was alive. Perhaps, no more kindly attention was required of them.

Carr, like his father before him, was a man of law. He was admitted to the Clements Inn in 1714, and in the following year, he bought the lease of his chambers at a cost of £130. He was probably an estate accountant too, and a clerk of sewers. He was sufficiently successful to be appointed Receiver General for Lincolnshire in 1741, when he was 53 years old. He passed away in the very same year. According to his will, he had become a very wealthy man. He owned land in forty-three areas of the Lindsey region of Lincolnshire, as well as land further south, in Boston and Skirbeck. His chambers in Clements Inn were left to his son, Thomas Carr, who also inherited some farms in Hertfordshire.

Augustus Brackenbury's grandfather, Thomas Carr (1720-71), was Carr Brackenbury's third son by his first wife, Ann Gace. He was a land agent, clerk of sewers and, for a number of years, the clerk of the peace. He was appointed the first Treasurer to the whole of the Parts of Lindsey, and he held this office for more than twenty years, from 1750 until his death in 1771. In 1747, he married Elizabeth Ostler, who had inherited Scremby Hall on the death of her uncle, John Moody. Elizabeth Ostler, Augustus's grandmother, died in 1760.

Thomas Carr Brackenbury and Elizabeth Ostler had three children: Carr Thomas, Charles and Anne. Charles, in whom we are most interested, was Augustus's father. He was born in 1750 and educated at Louth Grammar School and Jesus College, Cambridge. At the age of eleven, he was asked to be the page of the Duke of Ancaster at the coronation of George III and Queen Caroline. To mark the coronation, a charming portrait of him in his page's uniform was painted. From his early years, Charles had his heart set on joining the Church, and he became a career clergyman as well as a prosperous landowner. The sporting world appealed to him greatly; in particular, he enjoyed keeping a pack of harriers. Charles Brackenbury married Caroline or Anne Hairby, a member of a local family. One of the factors which may have caused Charles's death in 1816 was having one of his legs amputated, apparently 'owing to mortification'.

Charles's older brother, Carr Thomas, married a Mary Anne Vashel and they had three sons, and a daughter named Anna Maria, who was born in 1790. Charles's sister Anne, married a Captain Denshire of Stamford.

Before we move on to Augustus and his siblings, we shall briefly turn our attention to another line of the Lincolnshire Brackenburys, for the reason that Charles, Augustus's father, had a first cousin, who became well known in the Methodist circles of the time and, according to many commentators, was the most distinguished Brackenbury of them all. Robert Carr Brackenbury was born in 1752, at Panton House, near Wragby, in Lincolnshire, the son of Isabella Booth and Carr Brackenbury (b.1714), Augustus's great uncle. Isabella came from a wealthy family and was an heiress who had an income of £1,500 a year and a fortune of £40,000. In the year of Carr and Isabella's marriage, 1742, they bought Panton Hall, Wragby, from Carr's first cousin, Gace. They had ten children; but few survived beyond infancy, and this affected their son Robert greatly. Carr Brackenbury himself passed away when his son was only 11 years old.

Robert was educated at Felstead School, in Essex, and St Catherine's College, Cambridge, where he enjoyed horse-racing in his youth. As an undergraduate at Cambridge, Robert Carr Brackenbury had an intense religious experience which seriously affected his health and wellbeing. He had originally intended to become a clergyman but, at 24 years of age, he abandoned the idea of entering the Church and was instead introduced to Methodist ideas. He met John Wesley in 1776, when Wesley was an old man of 73 years. His associations with Wesley inspired Robert greatly; he set about building himself a house, but, more importantly, a chapel, at Raithby. Wesley soon paid a visit to Raithby and dedicated the chapel in July 1779. Robert became a Methodist preacher himself and enjoyed being in the confidence of John Wesley. Wesley apparently thought the world of him, saying at one time, "What is mine is yours, you are my brother, my friend."

Robert Carr Brackenbury married twice. His first wife, Jane, lost her life as the result of an accident in 1782. Some thirteen years later, he decided to remarry and a Leicestershire woman named Sarah Holland became his wife. She was also a very enthusiastic Methodist, and known to be 'a most excellent Christian woman'. Brackenbury and his wife were responsible for introducing Methodism to the Channel Islands in the 1780s. However, Robert's ministry on the islands encountered tremendous opposition. Nevertheless, he was a stubborn fellow, who knew that what he was doing was right, and he pursued his mission for a number of years. With John Wesley, Brackenbury travelled regularly overseas, as well as travelling widely across England, promoting Methodism.

Robert Carr Brackenbury was 65 years old when he died in August 1818. He was buried in Raithby church. He seems to have destroyed all the letters and papers that would have told us more about the true extent of his life's good works. Brackenbury died childless and his estate at Raithby became the property for her life of his widow Sarah, who was very much his junior. She lived until 1847. She continued to support Methodist causes in the Channel Islands and other areas where her husband had worked, and she also contributed to missions all over the British Isles and abroad. It was her interest in missionary work in Africa which led to there being a place in South Africa called Raithby.

★   ★   ★

We now turn to Augustus's generation and look at his many siblings. Augustus had four brothers and four sisters. Caroline was the eldest and she was born in 1782. She remained unmarried and died at Scremby in 1865. The eldest son Charles, born in 1783, came next. He became the rector of Aswardby. He married and produced a daughter, Janetta. Anne and George Brackenbury were born in 1785 and 1787 respectively, but they both died at a young age. Sophia Brackenbury was born in 1787. Like her elder sister Caroline, she was a spinster and also lived until her death at Scremby. To amuse themselves, the two old ladies would often be seen by the locals, spending an afternoon driving into Alford, in their carriage with an outrider. Henry was the next born, in 1789. He received an MA from Jesus College, Cambridge and became a clergyman. His life was as intriguing as that of his younger brother, Augustus, who was born three years later, in 1792. After the birth of Augustus, there would be another son born to the family, Evelyn, in 1793. He also gained a BA at Jesus College, Cambridge, in 1815. He lived in London for most of his life and died at his home in Park Villa, Regents Park. The last born of Charles and Caroline Brackenbury would be Louisa, who was born in 1795, but her life was comparatively short; she died at the tender age of eighteen, in 1813.

Charles, the eldest son, caused family controversy when he decided to marry his cousin, against the wishes of the family. He lost his inheritance as a result. It was, therefore, Charles Brackenbury's third son, Henry, who inherited Scremby Hall from his parents. After his spell at Cambridge University, he became Rector of Scremby and held this post between 1816 and 1862. He was also Vicar of Dunholme, between 1837 and 1849. In 1821, at the age of 32, he married Anne Atkinson. A native of Yorkshire, Anne Atkinson was a close friend of the poet Alfred Tennyson's sister Mary, and Anne was known as 'Georgiana' to the Tennyson family. It seems that Tennyson was a regular visitor to Scremby as he once wrote to his friend John Foster, "I have been flying about from house to house for a long time, and yours was delivered to me at a place called Scremby Hall in this county where I was making a morning call."

Henry was a sporty fellow, much like his father. As already noted, Charles Brackenbury had started a pack of harriers, and Henry continued the tradition after his father's death. In 1820, Henry replaced them with foxhounds and the pack was known as The Gillingham. Occasionally, Henry's love of sport took precedence over his public duties. The sexton would have to announce from the pulpit, on many a Sunday, that there would be no service that day because his Reverence had gone to the races. Henry had a fondness for gambling, and as he became increasingly debt ridden, he had to mortgage his inheritance of Scremby. At the time, he had no children, and the mortgage deed included a provision that, if he died childless, the mortgagee would inherit Scremby Hall.

His wife Anne had died childless, on the 11th of July 1858. A mausoleum in her memory, built in the grand gothic style, was erected by Henry in the grounds of Scremby Hall. However, worries about the conditions in the mortgage deed on Scremby constantly filled his thoughts, and just over a year later and in much haste, he married Julia Charlotte Hare, daughter of Robert Cropper, of Laceby House, near Grimsby. He was by now a man of seventy years, she a mere twenty-six-year-old. To complicate matters further, they were already related by marriage, as Henry's niece was married to her uncle. However, on 16th of August 1860, Julia dutifully produced a son and heir, Henry Charles Verschoyle Julius. In June 1861, Henry made a will, leaving his personal property and the estate in trust to his new wife for the duration of her life, and then to their son after her death. By December 1861, Julia had given birth to a daughter, named Julia Florence. Some six months later, Henry died aged 71 and he was buried with his first wife in the mausoleum at Scremby.

If Henry was a rather colourful character, his son (and Augustus's nephew), who was known as Verschoyle, was a chip off the old block, too. He was sent to Eton for his schooling and there he befriended the 'yellow Earl' of Lonsdale, who had a reputation for heavy drinking. Verschoyle succumbed to heavy bouts of drinking, too, during his lifetime. Despite these episodes, he became a Captain in the 3rd battalion Lincolnshire Regiment. On his twenty-first birth day, his mother disentailed the estate of Scremby Hall and handed it over to her son, renouncing any interest in the estate for the rest of her life. Having been given such a golden egg, Verschoyle, unfortunately, set about destroying what he had been given. He soon had a severe drink problem, which ate up a considerable amount of his wealth. He was a womaniser and lavished gifts which he could not afford. As a result, Scremby Hall was yet again mortgaged up to the hilt, with Verschoyle having borrowed the entire value of the estate. However, fortunately for him and to save further family embarrassment, his aunt on his mother's side, Miss Frances Cropper, who owned much of the land around Scremby Hall by the end of the nineteenth century, agreed to take on the mortgage of Scremby and by default became the owner of Scremby Hall in 1898. A year later, she was dead, but she left the estate to her two sisters, with Julia Brackenbury, who, forty years earlier, had renounced all interest in the Scremby estate, now inheriting two thirds of it. As for Verschoyle, he died unmarried at the Bridge Hotel, Newhaven, at the age of forty, leaving a mere £555. He was interred in the family mausoleum at Scremby. His death brought about the end of the male line of Scremby Brackenburys.

Verschoyle's sister, Julia Florence, married Frederick Oswald Lasseter, a Roman Catholic. It seems that none of the Brackenbury's of Scremby was present at their wedding in London. Julia lived most of her life at Scremby Grange; she died in 1919, and was buried at Scremby. Her daughter, Iris Clare, spent most of her life at Scremby Grange, died unmarried in 1984, and was also buried at Scremby.

★   ★   ★

Most Mynydd Bach residents of the 1820s knew little of Augustus Brackenbury's background; rumour had it that he may have been Irish or Jewish by birth. We now know that this assumption was incorrect. It is possible that his physical appearance led to this rumour. An anonymous and undated essayist once described the twenty-eight-year-old Augustus as being quite short in body, with black hair, mean looking grey eyes, a large forehead, a long nose and thick lips. He travelled around the countryside, wearing a silk hat, a long coat to his knees, a velvet waistcoat, carsimer trousers and white socks.

Augustus did not follow the Brackenbury family trait of being tall and fair, and this may have led to him being seen as the 'odd one out' of the family, according to a descendant of the family, Miss Diana Brackenbury of Horncastle, Lincolnshire. Augustus was not a name descended from generations of Brackenburys. It is thought that he was the only Brackenbury to bear that name.

Augustus was probably educated at a public school, either in Orme or at Louth, as were his brothers. However, he did not follow his brothers Charles, Henry and Evelyn and many of his cousins to Cambridge University. Many in the family became clergymen, and Augustus's cousin, Joseph, wrote a book of poetry *Natale Solum, and other poetical pieces* in 1810, but despite the fact that it was never published, the manuscript is to be found at the National Library of Wales in Aberystwyth.

Augustus may not have enjoyed a happy childhood because he seemed so very different to his other siblings. He may have been seen as a rebel, wanting to pursue his own interests and showing little enthusiasm for toeing the family line by attending university like his brothers, or by becoming an attorney or a clergyman, like many of the male Brackenburys. Augustus was an independent spirit and that quality would take him from the east coast of England to the west coast of Wales, to seek a meaning to his life.

## Chapter 4

# BRACKENBURY ARRIVES ON MYNYDD BACH

AUGUSTUS BRACKENBURY ARRIVED AT his newly acquired property on the Mynydd Bach in the autumn of 1819. He was now ready to make a new life for himself, and the Mynydd Bach area had the potential to allow him successfully to establish a shooting and hunting estate.

Having set up temporary lodgings in the coastal town of Aberystwyth, Brackenbury set about finding some local workmen to build houses on his Mynydd Bach land. Aberystwyth in the 1820s could be described as a genteel watering place. Its prosperity was not only based on commercial and industrial maritime activity, it was also a resort for the well-heeled gentry of mid-Wales. Marine baths had been opened in 1810, and by 1820 Assembly Rooms had been built. Aberystwyth boasted many Regency styled houses, which catered for the needs of the lesser gentry and prosperous yeomen farmers of the wider mid-Wales area. It was a picturesque place, with the sea and the scenery of the rolling hills lending a quite different aspect from the monotonously flat landscape of Lincolnshire with which Augustus had been familiar.

From a quarry on one of the hillsides of Mynydd Bach, Brackenbury's workmen began to extract stone on the 13th of December 1819. They carried on doing so until the middle of February 1820, when Brackenbury decided that enough stone had been sourced. Most of the men were then redeployed to start cultivating the boggy land of Mynydd Bach. Some men prepared the land, raising clods of peat to keep fires hearty; others started the process of building fences with the quarried stone and enclosing some of Brackenbury's newly acquired Crown land. This feverish activity on the mountain resulted in as many as fifty local men being employed by Brackenbury by the month of April 1820. Augustus was a willing employer; he had plenty of plans and was injecting a great deal of money into the local economy. At this early stage, it is uncertain whether the locals shared his view that he was doing a great deal of good in the area.

The honeymoon period of the initial few months was coming to an end. The local inhabitants began seriously to assess the stranger amongst them. Brackenbury, unaware of the growing, underlying tensions, decided to concentrate all his efforts on building dwellings. Towards the end April, carpenters started to prepare wood for the house in which Augustus himself would live. He already had a name in mind for the house: 'Green Meadow'; however, the proposed site of the house would not remind one of a typical meadow. No such land existed on Mynydd Bach. Brackenbury was, naturally, in something of a hurry to get this house built, as the journey backwards and forwards from Aberystwyth was rather long and tiresome.

By the first of May 1820, stonemasons had been employed and the work of erecting the walls of the house at 'Green Meadow' had begun. Barely a month later, good progress had been made and most of the walls were now about nine feet high. However, the night of the 25th of May brought about Brackenbury's first setback. After nightfall, most of the walls of 'Green Meadow' were knocked down by a group of unknown men. Two nights later, what remained of the walls was taken down further,

*Green Meadow was reduced to rubble in a similar fashion to this example from near Llyn Eiddwen today.*

leaving only foundations. The timber was set on fire too, and Brackenbury's first dream lay in ashes.

Augustus must have been rather baffled by this incident. After all, he'd been travelling backwards and forwards to the area for about six months, by this time. He was known by sight to most of the residents. He had found work for and paid wages to a good many of them over the past few months. Some of the locals must, he assumed, have had a hand in, or knowledge of, the actions that took place on those late May evenings. Therefore, on the discovery of the demolished walls, Brackenbury made his way to the local Justice of the Peace, to place an official complaint. The magistrate A T J Gwynne Esq heard Brackenbury's grievances. As he explained the situation to the Justice, it became clear that Augustus had already employed some detective skills of his own and had made some initial enquiries locally about the incidents. Having described the fashion in which his house had been completely demolished, he started to make some suggestions as to who the perpetrators might have been. These insinuations may have upset the Justice, as it seemed that perhaps Brackenbury was already doing the Justice's investigative work for him and forming conclusions which may have been wide of the mark. After all, Brackenbury was a newcomer to the area and knew little of the people and the way of life on the hills.

Augustus had discovered that some tools which had been used by his labourers in the construction of 'Green Meadow' had been left at night in the cottage of a man living nearby. These diligent workers would make sure that their tools were clean at the end of each working day. Two days after the burning of 'Green Meadow', on the morning of Monday 29th May, the labourers collected their tools as usual, only to find them covered in lime and earth, similar to that found where they had erected the enclosure fences.

The occupier of the cottage where the tools were regularly deposited was interrogated about the appearance of the tools by Brackenbury and his workmen. The householder was a simple man and he pleaded ignorance of the whole matter. Despite living in the cottage, he had no idea who had removed the tools, meddled with them and placed them back. He claimed to have been in bed during the incident and had not thought it strange to hear someone moving tools out of his cottage in the middle of the night. He certainly couldn't nor wouldn't put a name to any guilty person, as he hadn't seen anybody. Brackenbury, to be sure, could sense a local conspiracy arising against him.

Having listened to Brackenbury's account, the Justice of the Peace seemed totally unfazed. In fact, the law enforcement officer's advice to Brackenbury was to try to forget the episode and to do nothing more about the matter. He argued that to take the matter further would be a foolish move, as Brackenbury would '… be in a worse predicament than if [he] should let it rest unexamined'. Augustus Brackenbury must have been totally astonished at the magistrate's findings, but on this occasion, he decided to follow the magistrate's advice.

Monday, 29 May 1820, turned out to be another day to

forget in the life of Augustus Brackenbury. That day, he'd also been viewing the damage to his property at 'Green Meadow'. As he was leaving the ruins of his home and making his way back to Aberystwyth, he was assaulted with stones from behind, and several succeeded in hitting him. Having turned around to see who the perpetrators were, he caught sight of two youths, about fifteen years of age, running away at speed. Brackenbury gave chase and eventually caught one of them. He had no hesitation in frogmarching the offending youth towards the home of the nearest Justice of Peace. However, doubts as to the wisdom of such a move (after the previous advice from a Justice of Peace) must have entered Augustus's mind. He suddenly remembered that the Justice would not be at home for the rest of the day either, and he let the boy go. But before releasing the youth, Brackenbury ascertained the boy's name, and his father's name and address, at which they resided. It seemed that the boy was a farming neighbour of Brackenbury's. Interestingly, it was the boy's father, Mr Evans, who had originally been one of those who had advocated the Act of Parliament which had led to the enclosure of land on Mynydd Bach. However, once the Act had come into being and the farmer had discovered that the enclosure of land was in place only to cover various government expenses, he sought to do all in his means to prevent the enclosure of land on Mynydd Bach. The name of the other stone thrower was also discovered; he was the son of a tenant of one of the local freeholders.

As soon as the captive youth was released, he ran home and told his father what had happened. Farmer Evans, in a disgruntled fashion, made his way at once to the home of a Justice of Peace, Rev. Mr Evans, in this case, and filed a complaint against Augustus Brackenbury for the false imprisonment of his son. As a result, Brackenbury was summoned to appear before the magistrate, only to hear the youth deny categorically that he had thrown a stone at him. The Justice believed the evidence of the boy, and Brackenbury was duly fined 2s/6d for seizing the boy without cause. Despite Brackenbury pointing out to the magistrate that the youth had been running away from him when the incident happened, the magistrate failed to see this as sufficient evidence of a misdemeanour. If Augustus had not already been aware that everyone seemed to be conspiring against him, he was certainly conscious of it now.

The Mynydd Bach inhabitants vehemently disapproved of the fact that the land on which they had tried to make a meagre living for generations was now in the hands of an English gentleman from a faraway county. They failed to appreciate that Brackenbury had acquired the land by legal means and that this opposition (which they should have been showing towards those who'd proposed this specific enclosure, perhaps, or towards the government for selling the land at the outset) was being borne by a gentleman who had simply thought of the purchase of land as a sound investment. Alas, Augustus could only comfort himself with the thought that the attacks were not directed towards him personally. It is obvious that whoever had been in his shoes would have been treated in exactly the same way.

Stone throwing, with Augustus as the target, became

a common occurrence. Locals would lurk behind bushes, not far from roads that Augustus travelled upon, and bombard him with missiles. Often, Brackenbury felt in danger for his life. Grievances passed on by Augustus to the magistrate Rev. Mr Evans only brought about the far too often repeated riposte, that Englishmen were seldom known to thrive in country such as this.

Not only was Augustus being physically assaulted with stones but he was also the victim of the theft of his possessions. In a stable nearby, some leather pieces belonging to his horses, and some other gear were either stolen or damaged. Brackenbury had only been in the area for just over six months and had endured the most unfortunate experiences in recent weeks, ones which would have made a lesser man think seriously about leaving and selling up. However, Augustus was made of sterner material.

Barely a week after the complete demolition of 'Green Meadow', Augustus decided to rebuild his house. On this occasion, he took the precaution of employing watchmen, who would be constantly on guard, protecting the house night and day. The scheme seemed to be working well, for about three weeks, and progress on rebuilding the house was encouraging. The lull, however, was short-lived; on the night of the 26th of June, a mob of local men assembled near the building and started to fire at the house. Some ten men were inside, guarding it, at the time. The mob leader tried to summon one of the watchmen to come outside and surrender the building. Being brave and courageous, the watchmen ignored the request. Having lost this battle, the mob retreated, to plot further. They were still adamant that they were going to win the war.

The following day, Augustus Brackenbury visited the house of the Lord Lieutenant of Cardiganshire, Mr E Powell, Esq, and described in detail the previous night's disturbances. Disorder had evidently broken out on Mynydd Bach, and there were fanatics amongst the mob, who could cause grievous injury and even death to innocent people, he argued. Brackenbury suggested that some of the militia stationed in Aberystwyth could be redeployed to bring order back to Mynydd Bach and also assist in protecting Brackenbury's property. The Lord Lieutenant begrudgingly acceded to his request, but there were certain provisos. He wasn't prepared to force members of the militia to go to Mynydd Bach; they were at liberty to accept or decline the commission. Members of the militia who agreed to police Brackenbury's property on Mynydd Bach would be unarmed for the assignment and it was also expected that Brackenbury would pay the wages of the willing militia. All levels of society seemed to be quite unsympathetic to Augustus's plight.

By the 5th of July, some members of an unarmed militia, led by William Smith, had been recruited and were in place on Mynydd Bach, guarding Brackenbury's property. That night, the mob decided to pay another visit. The militia sat inside the building, whilst the mob fired several times from the outside. Sensing the seriousness of the situation, the militia began to have second thoughts about defending Brackenbury's property and, therefore, began to withdraw their support. They were being fired upon, night after night, and were still not allowed to defend themselves with their own weapons, despite further pleas to the Lord Lieutenant. Therefore, by Saturday, 8th of July, only three brave men remained on watch with Augustus. Most of the militia had returned to Aberystwyth.

On the night of Tuesday, 11th of July 1820, Augustus sat inside the nearly completed house, with three other men: William Smith, the only member of the militia who had remained loyal to Brackenbury, and two labourers, William Jones and Benjamin Davies. Between the hours of 11pm and 2am, some twenty to thirty men, bearing firearms, approached the building. What must have made this a rather peculiar sight to an impartial observer was the fact that many of these men were dressed in women's apparel, and others, who had failed to find a sufficient camouflage, had handkerchiefs about their faces. As the mob approached, Augustus was apparently asleep, but he was woken, when one of the mob called out for the Englishman and his supporters to leave the building. If they refused to do as was demanded, the mob planned to set the house on fire. Bravery deserted William Jones and William Smith; they were panic-stricken and immediately gave themselves up to the mob. Augustus, in turn, shouted at the mob out of the window, and exclaimed that this was his 'castle' and that he was entitled by law to defend it. One of the mob then responded by saying that, if that were the case, they would have no other option but to demolish the castle. Within minutes, iron implements were being hurled at the walls of the house. There was nothing further that Augustus could do, and so, having been persuaded by the ever loyal Benjamin Davies to go outside, he left the house – gun in hand.

Brackenbury approached the mob's ringleader and asked once more what they wanted. The ringleader replied that they wanted to take the house down. As this discussion was proceeding, Augustus was grabbed from behind by a couple of men, taken about twenty yards from the house and held captive there, whilst one of the men, Enoch Davies, ran into the house. Shortly afterwards, after other members of the mob had piled loose timber against the building, the whole house was set on fire by Davies, and was soon enveloped in flames. Firearms were discharged at the house, and it must have been quite a spectacle, watching a house, engulfed in flames, being shot at by men dressed up as women.

However, a far worse fate was to befall Augustus. At the height of the fire, he was manhandled by a few of the mob and held over a part of the fire, as if about to be roasted alive. He was asked repeatedly to leave Mynydd Bach and to promise never to return to this part of the world. Augustus, being strong willed and stubborn, could sense the metal buttons on his coat becoming so hot that they were beginning to melt. In order to save himself from a terrible death, he finally acquiesced and gave them the promise that they wanted to hear.

As the fire died down and it became safer for all to approach the building, many members of the mob dismantled the walls and found other combustible material inside the building to burn. It must have been a frenzy of activity, and all Brackenbury could do was look at the destruction and wonder why all this was happening to him and what he had done to deserve it.

As dawn broke, the mob scattered and Brackenbury was left to ponder his options. He was determined that he would be recompensed for the damage caused to his property, at the very least. On the following day, Wednesday, 12th of July, Augustus made a deposition in front of six Ilar and Geneu'r Glyn magistrates, including William Edward Powell, George Bonsall, Alban Thomas Jones Gwynne, William Lewis, John Nathaniel Williams and William Tilsley Jones. William Smith made a further deposition two days later, and this is his recollection of events:

Who upon his Oath said that he has been for the space of six weeks last past employed by Augustus Brackenbury Esquire at Green Meadow otherwise Waun Las in the parish of Llanrhystud as a labourer or servant. And this examinant further said that repeatedly during such period the premises belonging to the said Augustus Brackenbury have been in the night time visited by an assemblage of riotous and tumultuous persons armed with guns and that they have fired in the direction of the dwelling house at Green Meadow aforesaid, upon one of which occasions that is to say the night of Tuesday the 4th instant he heard distinctly the sound of balls passing through the air near the said dwelling house. That this examinant is quite satisfied that such sounds were produced by balls which had been fired from his having for many years last past served in the Royal Cardiganshire Militia. That from the reports of the guns and the flashes of light proceeding from their being fired this examinant believes the same to have been fired at a distance of about a hundred yards or thereabouts from the said dwelling house and from various directions surrounding the same, but that the persons who fired them did not on that occasion approach nearer. That on the night of Tuesday the 11th instant he this examinant together with Mr Brackenbury and two other persons whom he had employed to watch and protect his property were induced to suppose a similar attack would or might be made that night and that about one o'clock in the morning the other two men who had been sent out as scouts came in and stated "The mob are coming", upon which examinant immediately fastened the door and the men who were employed as scouts went into the loft and one of them (William Jones) when examinant followed them there he discovered talking to the mob through the window and one of whom said in Welsh "unless you come down we will burn you all". When William Jones replied "Stop a little and I will talk to the gentleman", meaning Mr Brackenbury. Immediately upon which the whole or a large portion cried "down with it, down with it" and gave three cheers, upon which William Jones left the window and spoke to Mr Brackenbury. Examinant upon looking through the window perceived an assemblage of from twenty to thirty persons, some of whom were disguised and armed with guns, standing in front of the house. That in a few minutes afterwards the mob or some of them said "Unless you come down in five minutes the house shall be set fire to". That after William Jones had spoken to Mr Brackenbury he went down and opened the door and went out and the mob or some of them immediately afterwards called out to examinant and the others to come out, upon which the examinant went out with a gun in his hand which was immediately seized by two of the mob and while the examinant was struggling with them others of them assailed him and he was obliged to forego his hold and give up his gun. They ordered the examinant to a particular situation in front of the house, and not move there-from at his peril, upon which the examinant retreated into the smoke arising from some pared land that was burning near to the house where he could not easily be discerned by the mob and he heard some of them enquire what was to become of him. While he was there he saw the mob gather the loose timber that was lying about the house in considerable quantities and throw it into the house where there was already a considerable blaze of light from the fire which had been fed by some straw and hay or some inflammable material thrown by the mob or some of them upon that previously used by Mr Brackenbury for his ordinary purposes. Then the blaze became general, and examinant retreated to a greater distance, to escape the mob who he repeatedly had heard threaten to kill him if they found him and soon afterwards the house and furniture and other effects which it contained were consumed, all of which took place within an hour after the first approach of the mob to the house. That his situation in the smoke in the pared land was about fifty yards distant from the house, and that when he saw the men through the window and was so seized by them upon his coming out, and in all the subsequent proceedings he was not able to discover any thing by which he can describe the features of the mob or give any correct description of their persons or dresses. That when the conflagration became general the mob shouted and continued throughout the act with great violence and noise, and some of them fired their guns

when examinant first went out. And this examinant
lastly said that Jenkin Lloyd, a carpenter employed by
Mr Brackenbury told this examinant on Tuesday last
that he had heard that an attack would be made that
night upon Mr Brackenbury's property.[4]

These depositions were forwarded to the then Home
Secretary, Viscount Sidmouth. Furthermore, at a meeting
held in the Talbot Inn, Aberystwyth on the 27th of July,
the above magistrates of Ilar and Geneu'r Glyn agreed to
offer a reward of one hundred guineas for information
leading to the conviction of an offender or offenders. If
any accomplices to the offence were to come forward,
then, they would be pardoned if they gave evidence.
This notice of an award would be inserted in the *London
Gazette*. Placing the notice in this particular publication
was indeed an interesting choice, as it was probably not
very well read by the mainly Welsh-speaking inhabitants of
Mynydd Bach. However, despite the generous reward and
offer of pardon for witnesses to the event, the perpetrators
of this particular arson attack remained undiscovered for
quite some time.

Despite promising to depart the county, whilst he
was being roasted above the embers of his home, on
the night of the 11th of July, Augustus Brackenbury had
no intention of going anywhere. Even his animals were
now being maimed, and it seemed that any association
with the Lincolnshire gentleman would be troublesome.
In the autumn, however, despite his setbacks, Augustus
set about building yet another cottage, only for it to be
demolished before it was completed. Then, on about the

4<sup>th</sup> of November, soon after the latest act of vandalism, he received a letter via Aberystwyth Post Office:

> Belfast Porridge Lane
> September 18<sup>th</sup> 1820

Sir,

We have been informed that you are going to erect another building on Mynydd Bach, be as expeditious as possibly you can; and as soon as it will be completed, we shall set sail the first favourable wind, and visit the said building; where we expect to have the same diversion as we had last summer at Green Meadow. It would be an addition to our pleasure if you will then be present, together with the cannibals and bloodsuckers D. J. Jenkins, John Hughes and James Hughes to partake of the diversion.

Yours &c.

Paddies

N.B. Remember us to your Sentry Boys and tell them to be watchful for fear.[5]

Augustus employed his detective skills once again and successfully managed to trace the name of the person who had written the letter: James Morris, a former clergyman of the Established Church, who had been thrown out of the Church, due to misconduct, and who subsequently spent his days keeping a school for the children of the neighbourhood. He was an itinerant fellow, who wandered from house to house, looking for his meals. Augustus's investigative work was certainly reaping dividends with regard to evidence, but it seemed that the magistrates still were not prepared to take his grievances or his information very seriously.

Brackenbury was undeterred by the latest setback, and, in December 1820, he employed eight men to raise stone from the local quarry, to build more houses. He also received some positive news, at the beginning of the New Year, regarding the hunt for the perpetrators of the previous July's attacks. There was a rumour that a witness had come forward to speak to the Justice of the Peace, Mr Williams of Ystradmeurig. Augustus wasted no time in contacting Mr Williams, but, unfortunately, he was to be disappointed with the result. The witness who'd been brave enough to come forward was Thomas Evans, the blacksmith. However, it soon became apparent that Mr Evans's life had been threatened, and that he was in danger, and so he decided that he was not prepared to give any further evidence. Another glimmer of hope of justice for the Englishman had been extinguished.

By the 14th of March 1821, enough stone had been quarried, and, ten days later, masons started to erect some more buildings. Work began on two cottages, and by the end of April, the walls of one of the cottages were nine feet high, whilst the other cottage had seven-foot-high walls. However, on the night of May 1st, all the hard work came to nothing, when yet another mob assembled and destroyed the cottages. Brackenbury had not employed anyone to keep watch over these cottages overnight, as he'd already given notice locally that they were going to be built. The proposed cottages were in close proximity to other, occupied, cottages, and it is possible that he assumed that they didn't need to be guarded. Soon after the destruction of the latest cottages, Brackenbury enquired of the neighbours whether or not they had heard any stones falling on the night in question. Augustus was not surprised to hear the now common response, that the locals had heard nothing because they were fast asleep in their beds.

But Brackenbury still had the events of the previous summer on his mind. In April, he once again circulated amongst the local magistrates the fruits of his own investigations into the matter. It seems that the Justices of the Peace were getting rather tired of seeing and hearing from Brackenbury, as only one of them, W T Jones Esq took any notice of his latest evidence. This magistrate suggested to him that he should take the advice of a counsel, with regard to the letter received from the 'Paddies'. Augustus did as was advocated, and went back to Mr Jones in due course, only for the magistrate to refuse to read the counsel's advice. Instead, the magistrate proposed to Augustus that he should seek the advice of another Justice, Mr G Bonsall (someone who had already ignored Augustus's original research). It was indeed a case of going round and round in circles for Augustus and he was getting absolutely nowhere.

However, another glimmer of hope appeared on the horizon on May 4th, 1821, when Augustus was told that an unknown person had approached another magistrate with information. This informant had told W T Jones

JP that, on the 26th of June 1820, he happened to be in Cardinan, near Mynydd Bach, between ten o'clock and twelve midnight, when he saw three men leave a house. For some inexplicable reason, this witness had then hidden himself behind a bush and observed the house. The informer witnessed the cobbler, Jac y Crydd, calling out from the front of the house of Evan Rees. Rees had come to the window and enquired who was with Jac and where were they going. Jac replied that his companions were Jac Rhos Goch and Tom Ffos-pomp-pren and that they were on their way up to Mynydd Bach, to take the Englishman's house down. Evan Rees offered his servant (yet another Jac) as a reinforcement, and they all went in the direction of the mountain, via the farm of Facwn. At last, Brackenbury had a lead, but, more importantly, the witness was certain that he hadn't been seen and therefore could not be intimidated into retracting his story.

These events eventually brought about a warrant for the arrest of Jac y Crydd, on the 5th of May. He was brought before the magistrate W T Jones Esq, who confined him to a prison cell for two days. With proceedings beginning to go in Brackenbury's favour at long last, another two warrants, for the arrest of Jac Rhos Goch and Tom Ffos-pomp-pren, were submitted. Both men were brought before magistrates on the 7th of May, with Jac y Crydd's situation being reviewed on the same day. However, it was decided by the Justices to let Jac Rhos Goch go free (apparently he was a tenant of one of the magistrates, John Nashe Williams Esq, and couldn't possibly have been guilty of such a deed). It was decided that Tom Ffos-pomp-pren could have his freedom also (as he was the tenant of a near relation of the same magistrate). Jac y Crydd was not as fortunate (he evidently was not on friendly terms with any magistrates); he was remanded in custody and waited to have his circumstances fought over another day.

Later on, moves were made to summons Evan Rees and his son. It seemed that, at last, the tide of justice was not only turning Brackenbury's way but flowing at a rate of knots. Many meetings were held, discussions were conducted, memories, which seemed to have failed many of the locals, stirred. Slow progress was made, with Evan Rees being questioned about the carriage of some lime, at around that time. Brackenbury also attempted to persuade the brave men who had stayed with him at 'Green Meadow' on that fateful night to return for questioning. However, despite all this progress, Jac y Crydd was the only suspect who remained in prison.

Most of the men now being questioned about this affair were brought in front of two magistrates, W T Jones and J N Williams, on Saturday, 12th of May. Evan Rees denied that the two Jacs and Tom had been anywhere near his house on the night in question. Evan Rees's son did exactly the same, on oath, and their testimony was believed and, henceforth, Jac Rhos Goch, Jac the servant and Tom were duly acquitted. Further fascinating developments ensued, when Jac y Crydd now turned to being a witness. He was asked about the large assembly of people on Mynydd Bach and the firing of shots in June 1820. He denied all knowledge of these occurrences, whilst standing in front of the magistrates. However, he had previously related a totally contrary story to Jenkin Humphrey, the gaoler of Aberystwyth.

In Jac y Crydd's account of the events of the 26th of June 1820 that he had given to the gaoler, he admitted that he had been in the company of Jac Rhos Goch and Tom Ffos-pomp-pren on that particular night. They had heard some shots and seen a large group of people, some mile and a half away from them. However, it seems that Jac y Crydd invented this account so that he could be released from prison. Other alleged witnesses to the events came forward, but all to no avail. Brackenbury began to consider that he'd probably have a better chance of justice were he to proceed against these perpetrators on the other side of Offa's Dyke. In truth, the likelihood of persuading the judicial system to consider this was remote.

Other new witnesses appeared on the horizon from time to time. On Monday 14th of May, Charles Lloyd deposed an oath before the magistrate Mr Bonsall. Mr Lloyd had been in conversation with a tailor, David Jones of Lledrod, in the home of a miner, Morgan Lewis, in Llanafan. David Jones had told Charles Lloyd that there were four hundred men willing to take the oath before two local magistrates and two counsellors from London, if necessary, that '… there shall not be any farms or houses built on Mynydd Bach, but what they shall be pulled down, without any poor man shall come, then he shall build a house and make a field, and we will help him'. David Jones had also mentioned the Brackenbury 'roasting' incident too, bragging that '… we held him until he was half roasted the time before, and the next time we shall roast him until he is dead'.

The locals not only objected to the fact that Brackenbury had purchased common land, but they also disliked his Englishness and his wealth. The above statement suggests that, if a poor local man wanted to build a house for his family and enclose some land around it on Mynydd Bach, there would be no objection locally. Brackenbury's perceived wealth annoyed the locals, who found life hard to bear, toiling to make a difficult living in an uncompromising and hostile terrain for farming. Augustus was also very much an outsider, an Englishman. English represented the voice of the authority.

David Jones, the tailor, became the latest subject of Augustus Brackenbury's enquiries. On Thursday, 17th May, Augustus travelled to Llanbadarn Fawr, a village just outside Aberystwyth, hoping that a magistrate would be on hand to question David Jones about the latest evidence. No magistrate appeared and the clerk to the magistrates, Mr James Hughes, informed Brackenbury that no warrant had been issued to request David Jones to appear before magistrates for questioning. Instead, the magistrates wished to see the men who had kept watch with Brackenbury on the fateful night. Those brave men, however, had dispersed to safer counties, such as Pembrokeshire. They no longer wanted any association with the Englishman of Mynydd Bach as it was deemed to be ill-fated.

Whilst all the legal wrangling was proceeding slowly, the boggy landscape of Mynydd Bach was yielding its annual harvest of peat. Much of this land was now owned by Brackenbury, but there was little that he could do, when hundreds of peat poachers descended on his land. Brackenbury tried to conciliate on this matter and requested that each person pay a shilling to come onto his private land. Everyone refused to pay, arguing that, if they paid one shilling one year, then Brackenbury could charge as much as he liked the following year. Augustus was rather perturbed that so many pensioners were persistently cutting peat on his land. He complained a great deal about a certain Evan Tobias, a sprightly pensioner, who apparently came all the way from Aberystwyth just to cut peat on his land.

Brackenbury also thought that some of the pensioners might prove to be rather useful to him. A pensioner named Roberts was employed to try to infiltrate the locals and find out the persons responsible for burning down his cottages. Augustus was getting rather desperate by now. Roberts regarded the one hundred guineas that Augustus paid him for this 'work' as blood money, and, therefore, another Brackenbury idea came to an abrupt end.

The attacks continued. A mob of between ten and fifteen persons took down a building which measured thirty-five square yards and had walls of around six feet in height. The mob was also becoming far more daring; this particular raid took place whilst Brackenbury's workmen were in chapel, at about nine o'clock at night. When two of his workmen were leaving the chapel, they heard the noise of falling stones, and hurried back to the site, which was about a mile and a quarter away. As they approached, they were spotted by the mob, which quickly dispersed in various directions.

This latest episode of unruliness led Brackenbury to

conclude that '... my estate is situated in the midst of the most desperate characters, who commit all kinds of depredations with impunity. The encroachers on the Freeholders' right of Common are so numerous, and so lawless, that they aid and assist each other to enclose the waste lands, and to keep possession thereof'.

Despite this, Augustus, at times, had some sympathy for the inhabitants amongst whom he attempted to reside. He was of the opinion that the cost of timber for building a cottage was far too high. Few native trees for wood for house building were to be found on Mynydd Bach. The cost of this basic requirement reduced the inhabitants to extreme poverty, which disabled them from cultivating the land that they had enclosed. Brackenbury observed that the locals, who enclosed land, would try to forge a living for only about two or three years. They would then abandon the place and let the cottage fall into ruin, with the land then reverting back to its uncultivated state. The cost to the parish was extreme; so many cottagers fell foul of the system, due to the lack of funds. Far too many were trying to make a living on far too little land.

Brackenbury argued that improving the land by cultivating it progressively was the answer to Mynydd Bach's problems. Advancement could be made if cottages were built to be rented out cheaply to locals, which would then result in the alleviation of the present poor living conditions. The pressure on the local parishes to support these needy people would then be reduced significantly. Augustus had thought a great deal about the economic future of Mynydd Bach. He envisaged having an estate where everyone would work and live together in harmony, sharing the prosperity gained.

It was but a pipe dream, unfortunately, and Brackenbury admitted that, at times, he understood why the locals were up in arms and so vehemently opposed to what he was trying to achieve. The cottagers, who had already established themselves on the mountain before Brackenbury's arrival, had built their own cottages and had enclosed some land around them. However, as we've already seen, unless the cottagers had been in residence for over two decades, the land did not legally belong to them. They then saw their common land sold to and colonized by a stranger. Augustus did have an understanding of the misfortunes of his neighbours.

Nevertheless, Augustus also regarded the peasantry of Mynydd Bach as deceitful, treacherous and given to falsehood. He was convinced that they lied under oath, although the magistrates tried to persuade him otherwise. His opinion of Cardiganshire was that '… this County is now labouring under a dreadful and deplorable want of morality and civilization'. He also felt that the magistrates '… should be entreated to be more diligent in assembling and hearing the several informations and complaints'.

Cardiganshire's magistrates may have been unwilling or unable to resolve Brackenbury's desperate situation, but he hoped that the Home Secretary would be more sympathetic. He wrote to Viscount Sidmouth on the 16th of June 1821, detailing all that had happened to him since his arrival on Mynydd Bach. The local magistrates' actions and inactions were noted, and at the end of his very successively, have Buildings been erected by me and destroyed, in spite of every precaution by Mobs riotously assembled and in most instances disguised and armed — I have frequently been assaulted with Stones; my Dwelling has repeatedly been fired at with Ball. I have been informed not in consequence of my own investigation only but from anonymous Threats conveyed to me by Letter, that the injuries which I received were the effects of a general Conspiracy consolidated by an unlawful Oath against me as an intruder, and that not my Property only but my life would be endangered; Information on Oath which I have been able to obtain has been met by the most unblushing perjury and the peasantry seem to have been encouraged in their Outrages, and in the effrontery with which they defend themselves on any occasion by an opinion which it appears impossible to remove from their minds that the Magistrates of the County and not cordial in their desire to bring the Offenders to justice —

These Causes render all my Attempts at redress by the ordinary means unavailing; and unless I am entitled in your Lordships consideration to some extraordinary protection from His Majesty's Government, I fear I must submit to be an example in the 19th Century of a Subject of this Realm, without the means of prevention or redress, deprived of a valuable Property by open and lawless force.

I subjoin an appendix containing a detail of some of the Injuries and acts of violence I have suffered — an illustration of the difficulties I have to contend against in the perjury of Witnesses and the consequent inadequacy of the local Magistracy or the existing Law to protect me, containing also at the end a proposal of some measures which I have ventured to suggest to your Lordship as likely to afford me some relief. Respectfully and earnestly entreating your Lordships Attention to my case, I have the honor to subscribe myself

Your Lordships obedient humble Servant

Augustus Brackenbury

To the right honorable
Lord Viscount Sidmouth
&c      &c      &c

*Brackenbury's Letter.*
*The National Archives, ref. HO40/16.*

81

lengthy letter, he requests that the Home Secretary send a deployment of soldiers to Aberystwyth, to keep order in Cardiganshire. As we've already seen, this was not an excessive request; a detachment of the 38th Regiment of Foot had been sent to Aberystwyth in 1817, to protect the commissioners acting under the same Enclosure Act of 1815.

Augustus was evidently making little progress with regard to his ambition for a shooting and hunting estate on Mynydd Bach. Whenever one of his buildings was erected, it was soon demolished. The perpetrators, despite growing evidence against them, remained at large. The magistrates stood in the middle of the road, fearful of stepping one way or the other, lest they be run over by one of the parties. In eighteen weary months, Brackenbury had wasted his time, had spent more than half of his inheritance, and only had some demolished walls to show for it. Was it not time to call it a day and return to England?

Reluctantly, he did so and spent the next four years in England. However, he deplored the thought that the inhabitants of Mynydd Bach had gained some sort of victory over him. He comforted himself in the knowledge that, despite everything, he was still the legal and rightful owner of 856 acres of former Crown land in Cardiganshire.

## Chapter 5

# BRACKENBURY RETURNS

AUGUSTUS RETURNED TO MYNYDD Bach, sometime in 1825. During his previous sojourn on Mynydd Bach, he had often referred to his house at 'Green Meadow' as being his castle. Indeed, this time, he was planning to build a proper castle, which would be surrounded by a protective moat.

Once again, stone for the castle was quarried locally, at Pen y Foel, by men who were willing to be in his employment. Despite the events of the early 1820s, it seems that many of the local inhabitants had no real qualms about, or objections to, taking employment and pay from Brackenbury. The castle, which was completed in April 1826, was situated at Troed y Foel, at the foot of a hillock. Brackenbury gave it the name of Castell Talwrn (Talwrn Castle). It was quite an extraordinary structure for this part of the world. It comprised a round tower (for keeping watch over the surrounding countryside for saboteurs) and an additional building, which had narrow doors and windows. A square moat, eight feet wide and three feet deep, surrounded the structure. Access to the castle was via a drawbridge, which would be lifted at night, for security purposes. The site was said to cover about two square acres, which makes it a rather large castle compound indeed.

All seemed to be progressing well, initially. The external structure of the castle was upright, and in order to keep it that way, Brackenbury went to Shrewsbury, to find men who he could trust to the keep the castle, its contents and Augustus himself secure. Brackenbury returned from Shrewsbury on the 13th of April 1826, in order to take up residence with his new loyal workforce. The twelve workmen he employed were craftsmen and they would work within the castle confines and cultivate the surrounding land, as required. They were led by John Whittal, a personal attendant, who was assigned solely to look after Augustus. Augustus may have regarded John Whittal as a personal assistant; however, the local inhabitants' opinion of him was that he was a bully. A local woman, Elizabeth Davies (the wife of Benjamin Davies, one of Brackenbury's trustworthy workers from 1820), was employed to keep house for the men and look after the castle. It seemed that, at last, with an eight foot wide moat to protect him, the tide in Augustus's fortune on Mynydd Bach was beginning to turn for the better.

Alas, it was soon apparent that it was not. Trouble was afoot as soon as he was installed in Castell Talwrn. This time, it had nothing to do with demolishing the walls of newly erected buildings. The local inhabitants were determined to ensnare him by some other means. The following petition was drawn up by the inhabitants of the hundred of Ilar and sent to their local magistrates; it is dated 12 June 1826 and it clearly shows the grievances that the locals held against Augustus in April and May of that particular year:

> Whereas the following is a true statement of Augustus Brackenbury and his men's barbarity and illegal proceedings on Mynydd Bach previous to the demolishing and pulling down his castle and fortress on the said mountain, is submitted to your wise consideration.
>
> On Sunday 23rd of April as Elizabeth Jones was going from her service on a visit to her parents, passing near his castle, she was dragged by Brackenbury and one of his bullies with imprecations of throwing her into a deep moat which surrounds the castle. Her cries being heard by a man who happened to be near went to her assistance, whom they also abused in a most barbarous manner holding a musket to his face, threatening to shoot him. But at last struck him with the muzzle of *it* and cut a deep gash on his upper lip. Had he not been at hand at the time most probable they would have committed more violence and violated her person. On the 27th April a poor boy happening to be near was pursued by Brackenbury and the poor boy in order to escape the pursuit threw off his wooden shoes, which he carried to his castle and never returned them to the poor fatherless boy. On Sunday May 7th and the two following Sundays mangled and destroyed the turf of Elizabeth Morgan, and carried off at the same time a few dry bushes which she'd fixed near her dwelling to dry linen &c. upon. May 10th stealing the turf of Joshua Davies and breaking his cart. On the same day Lewis Davies was also abused on his return with his cart and horses loaden with turf they attacked, jostled,

threatened, and pursued him three fourth of a mile and stole a sack from him which they never returned – May 20<sup>th</sup> John Jones son of David Jones was also most shamefully abused by dragging and threatening him and throwing his cart and horse into a bog. The young man's father who had no concern in the late tumult is now in goal and his children without a mother are under pressing wants; and also a poor widow is now in the house of correction without any cause whatever, except it be ye false oaths of his bullies he and his banditti being the greatest reprobates he could find in England and elsewhere have committed such atrocities on scores of individuals (too numerous to mention) by destroying their turf &c. that it calls aloud for vengeance. This is but a short sketch of Brackenbury and his bullies barbarity and cruelty of *Mynydd Bach*. No person could pass and repass without being insulted, assaulted and pursued and shot after; and all the diabolical practices committed (in particular) on the Sabboth days – by carrying fire arms, shovels and other implements suitable for their evil purposes – such cruelties and barbarities irritated the inhabitants (and no wonder if rightly considered) to demolish and pull down his castle and his strong holds. We are sorry to say that our Justices seem to be partial to Brackenbury's conduct. Had they listened to the complaint of the suffering individuals his castle might have been still standing. As we can have no Justice done at *Aberystwyth* we hope and pray that you Honoured Sir will exert yourself in our behalf to overthrow of ye tyrant, and his adherents at Aberystwyth; that peace and tranquillity may still abound instead of tyranny and oppression. No provocation or molestation whatever was committed by any one of the inhabitants previous to the pulling down of his castle. If some way or other be not contrived to put a stop to his atrocities it is to be feared further mischief and serious consequences will ensue.

Servants and sufferers in the Hundred of Ilar.[6]

These accounts of the events on Mynydd Bach were becoming well known by word of mouth throughout the whole of Cardiganshire and further beyond. The stories were also being read in the newspapers. A letter from a certain 'Verax' in the *Carmarthen Journal* of 11 August 1826, page 3, details the first incident in the above petition. It was David Evans who discovered the girl as she was about to be thrown into the moat. Evans, who was then allegedly struck in the face by Brackenbury, brought the case in front of magistrates and, according to 'Verax', Augustus was made to pay compensation of one guinea to the girl and £2.10s to David Evans.

Augustus vehemently objected to anyone who trespassed onto his land, for whatever reason. This is probably why he got himself so agitated at the sight of the servant girl. Many of the incidents mentioned in the above petition relate to the trespass of people trying to cut turf and peat on Brackenbury's land. John Jones was the name of the youth in the 27th of April incident. 'Verax' also claims in his published letter that Brackenbury's workmen demolished the turf stacks of poor people. Augustus had failed to appreciate that previous generations had been freely allowed to cut peat for fuel on his the land, as it was common land. Augustus's workforce retaliated by bruising the turf collected beneath their feet and then throwing it back into the turbaries. They would often do this on a Sunday, whilst the local people were worshipping in chapel or church. In this religious area, such actions would have proved to be very controversial.

As the month of May 1826 came to an end, it ushered in Augustus Brackenbury's bleakest time on Mynydd Bach. On the 23rd of May, Augustus, accompanied by John Whittal, travelled to Aberystwyth on business, and they decided to stay there overnight. News that both men had gone away to town spread quickly amongst the inhabitants on the mountain. That night, a plan was hatched, which would show the enormous strength and determination of people who were convinced that they had been wronged.

The following morning, 24 May, the inhabitants were out on the moor, cutting peat as usual. An ordained clergyman, Mr Lewis of Pant y Barwn, rode from bog to bog, informing the peat-cutters of the plan, which would be implemented later that day, and warned them to be ready for action. At some point that morning, once Mr Lewis had done his rounds, a horn was sounded across Mynydd Bach by a youth named Siaci Ifan y Gof. The horn was the signal for all inhabitants to assemble at appropriate points on the mountainside. A couplet written at the time is still remembered to this day:

> *Fe chwythwyd yr udgorn*
> *ar ben yr Hebrysg fawr.*
> *Daeth mwy na mil o ddynion*
> *ynghyd mewn hanner awr.*

(The horn was sounded on Hebrysg fawr.
More than a thousand men came together
in half an hour)

The monthly newspaper, *Seren Gomer,* published
nationally in Wales (December 1826, page 377), reported
that the number of men, women and children assembled
on the mountainside was a force of about six hundred.
Whatever the true figure, it was an impressive body of
people.

The largest mob appeared on the mountain between
Troed y Foel, where the castle was located, and Tan yr
Afon. Most of the protestors stayed there to look on,
whilst the leading figures in this unfolding campaign, Alun
Jones, Penlanowen, David Jones, Pantyrwyn, and one
other (one each from the parishes of Llanrhystud, Lledrod
and Llangwyryfon) were delegated to go to speak to the
men who had remained in the castle, or the pond, as it was
called by the locals. They warned, in no uncertain terms,
the men and woman holed up inside the castle to leave
within the hour, or they would be burnt alive, along with
the castle itself.

Four terrified men were in residence inside the castle,
their minds in a quandary with this latest threat. Three
of them were adamant that their best option was to
leave in haste and hope for the best. They gathered as
many of their belongings as they could, threw down the
drawbridge, shook hands begrudgingly with the leaders of
the mob, and as had been already been promised to them,
were allowed free passage to where ever they wanted to
go. The Englishmen decided it wise to go in the direction

of Aberystwyth and were met on the way by Brackenbury and Whittal, who were going homewards. The latter were informed that there were large numbers of unstable people protesting outside the castle. Therefore, all five, somewhat prudently decided to travel towards Aberystwyth. Elizabeth Davies, the housekeeper remained in the castle, along with another man, John Clark.

As soon as the drawbridge was down, the impatient mob rushed in. Much amusement was had in throwing bedding and furniture into the moat. Doors were torn down and floors pulled up and everything moveable was thrown into the moat, until it was full to the brim. The demolition of the castle then began, with banging and clanging being heard for miles. However, it seems that the mob did not carry out their threat to burn the building. Once significant damage was done, the mob returned to their cottages along the hillsides. Later on, the men of Trefenter (who were very hot-headed, by all accounts) took over, and looted everything. By the following morning, virtually nothing was left of Castell Talwrn. The castle had all but vanished into the thin moor air.

A fearful Augustus appeared before the magistrates Thomas Williams and Richard O Powell in Aberystwyth, five days after the riot, on the 29th of May. He entered into a bond of £50 to appear at the Court of Great Sessions in Cardigan, in order to prefer a bill of indictment against David Jones and his son John (otherwise known as Dafydd Ifan y Gof and Siaci Ifan y Gof, the horn blower), for taking part in the riot. John Clark, who'd remained in the castle until the end and had witnessed the whole incident, also entered a £25 bond and, a few weeks later, Benjamin Davies, a labourer, entered into a bond for the appearance of Elizabeth Davies, his wife, to give evidence as a witness in the same trial.

Enquiries were progressing well and, at the beginning of June, in response to nationwide publicity, soldiers were drafted into the area. However, they found it difficult to arrest anyone as many of the inhabitants had fled to the homes of relatives. It seemed that no one was sleeping in their own bed any longer. David Jones (Dafydd Ifan y Gof) fled to Aberystwyth, but was arrested in a public house there, and at around the same time, his son Siaci was arrested, too. Dafydd Ifan was a forty-year-old, who lived at Bwlchymynydd, in the parish of Llanrhystud, whilst his fourteen-year-old son was in service with a farmer, yet another Dafydd Jones, at Ty'nwern, in the locality.

At some point before the 12th of June (which was the date of the petition), father and son were transported to Cardigan gaol. However, whilst those transporting them to Cardigan refreshed themselves at the New Inn tavern, in the parish of Llangrannog, the son, despite being handcuffed, managed to escape and fled. The father, however, was much less fortunate, and remained in prison until the hearing of the Great Sessions. But he was not the only resident of Mynydd Bach languishing in the gaol. It appears that Catherine Jones of Penbryn had appeared before magistrate Thomas Williams on 17th June, on the charge of riotous assembly on 24th of May. She was granted bail of £100, together with two sureties of £50 each from Thomas Jones, a grocer from Aberystwyth, and

David Rowlands, a farmer from Llanrhystud. She would be recalled to the next Great Sessions at Cardigan. It seems that only one man and one woman out of six hundred persons had been successfully identified, charged and detained in gaol as a result of the incident.

Details of proceedings from that date onwards are somewhat confusing. One account from the time, which was found in a manuscript in the National Library of Wales, suggests that David Jones (Dafydd Ifan y Gof) was indeed brought before the Court of Great Sessions in Cardigan, where he was tried before Sergeant Samuel Heywood, who was a Judge on the Carmarthen circuit of the Court of Great Sessions at the time. The court hearing must have been rather bizarre. The monolingual Welsh speaker Dafydd Ifan y Gof had to listen to evidence spoken against him by the witnesses in English. The same was true of the jury, – nine out of ten of the jury members were also monolingual Welsh, sitting in court rather bemusedly, neither understanding a word of the evidence nor the directions of the Judge. This being the case, it was reasonably suggested to Judge Heywood that the evidence of the principal witnesses, at least, should be translated into Welsh. Judge Heywood, however, would have none of it; he insisted that, by law, all proceedings in a court of justice should be in the English language. In the December 1826 edition of the monthly newspaper *Seren Gomer*, it is revealed that this decision provided great mirth for the bilingual occupants of the court. However, the major language obstacle proved to be most favourable to Dafydd Ifan y Gof in the end. As the vast majority of the jury did not understand a word of the evidence, the case was thrown out and the detainee was acquitted and released.

Another account (dated 1899 however) of the time recounts events differently. This account was relayed by a certain H Tobit Evans to the Lampeter-based *Brython* weekly newspaper and puts a different angle on the proceedings that followed Dafydd Ifan y Gof's incarceration. According to Tobit Evans's account (dated from 22 September 1899, through to 10 November 1899), it was someone merely known as the 'ringleader' who was tried before the Great Sessions, and these sittings began on 21 August 1826. This ringleader was tried in front of Michael Nolan and Robert Matthew Casbard, who were in fact Judges of the Brecon circuit at the time. This could indeed suggest that Brackenbury had won his argument in getting the trial transferred to another circuit, as he was of the strong opinion that most of the people of Cardiganshire were already prejudiced against him and that any trial which involved him would be deemed to be unfair.

Dafydd Ifan y Gof was present at the trial on 21 August, but was tried separately from the ringleader, it seems. A true bill was sought against Dafydd Ifan, at which he pleaded not guilty. A certain Mr Russel and the London-based Attorney General, Sir William Owen (a member of the Owen family from Orielton, Pembrokeshire), conducted the prosecution. The defence was presided over by an eminent barrister, Edward Vaughan Williams. John Clark, as one of Brackenbury's men holed up in the castle when it was threatened, was called as a witness, and he eloquently described being in the castle with Elizabeth Davies in the moments before the mob broke in.

The court case soon descended into farce, however. John Clark initially said on oath that he recognised Dafydd Ifan y Gof as one of those men who had broken into the castle with the mob. Having been aggrieved to hear this, Dafydd Ifan started to curse and get rather flustered. He then proceeded to cross examine John Clark himself, despite his experienced counsel being present. Many offensive comments were exchanged, but eventually John Clark did admit that he'd probably only seen Dafydd Ifan in the crowd. This was the death knell to the prosecution case. Elizabeth Davies was another chief witness in the case, and the defence succeeded in discrediting her evidence, too. It seems that she was not a religious woman and, therefore, the oath that she'd voiced was deemed worthless. According to newspaper reports, a part of her testimony was also missing. With so much questionable evidence, the jury duly returned a verdict of not guilty on Dafydd Ifan y Gof.

By the month of August 1826, despite the disappointing result of the court proceedings, Brackenbury's fortunes were in the ascendancy again. As a result of a writ of enquiry, the Court of Great Sessions awarded Brackenbury £250 in damages against the inhabitants of the hundred of Ilar (that is, the people of Mynydd Bach) for the destruction of his houses, fences and other property. This was a substantial amount of money for the citizens of Ilar to find; it was to take the form of taxes, payable over a period of time. As a result of this financial penalty and the fear that they'd have to compensate Brackenbury again, perhaps, his mountain neighbours finally left Brackenbury to his own devices. Subsequently, Augustus also learnt that the magistrate Thomas Williams had decided to charge the seventy-five-year-old William Williams, for his part in a riot. He would be indicted at the Court of Great Sessions, which were to be held at Cardigan in April 1827. The *Carmarthen Journal* of 10 October 1826 states that many more rioters were in line to be arrested over the incidents. Several constables attempted to arrest one of the rioters, a blacksmith called Jac Gof, who lived at Yr Esgair. The story goes that the constables came on horseback in the early hours of a Monday morning and found Jac in bed. An old man called Lewis raised the alarm that Jac was going to be incarcerated. Sergeant Phillips, a former volunteer in the Irish troubles, was informed and immediately organised a rescue. He got to Yr Esgair in time to see the bound blacksmith being taken away on horseback. Sergeant Phillips and one other waylaid the constables as they were making their way up Esgair hill. The constables were attacked with a spade handle, which made one of the constables drop his pistol, which discharged, wounding one of them. The constables fled and Jac Gof, Yr Esgair was once again a free man.

Augustus abandoned all hope of ever receiving justice. He decided to spend less time in the Mynydd Bach area. He travelled back and forth between England and Mynydd Bach in the intervening years, but he returned once more in 1828, for what would turn out to be his last extended period on Mynydd Bach. He built another home, this time on the lower slopes of Mynydd Bach, on land called Pant-y-gwair. Interestingly, he called it Cofadail Heddwch, which translated into English means a monument to peace. The name of the new dwelling evidently struck a chord with his neighbours, as he was allowed to live there quite undisturbed. He was also making plans to leave the area completely, and spent most of the year or so that followed in parcelling up his land, in order for it to be sold.

Brackenbury's troubles touched many other lives and those who had stood by him suffered similar fates. Benjamin Davies and his wife Elizabeth, who were so loyal to Augustus, saw their home and furniture set on fire and totally destroyed, some time before the end of October 1826. Despite the fact that they were of these hills originally, they moved out of the area and settled in the neighbourhood of Shrewsbury. Dafydd Ifan y Gof, who was tried, unsuccessfully, for rioting and for damaging Augustus's property, died some eight years after the events, at the age of forty-eight. His son, Siaci, the horn-blower, lived to the ripe old age of eighty-seven, and died on 26 June 1897. Once he had grown out of his youthful ways, he became sexton and gravedigger at Llangwyryfon. No doubt it was his reminiscences which led to the story of the little Englishman being retold in the newspapers and magazines of the tail end of the nineteenth century.

The war was over. There were winners and losers, but no-one had come out of the past ten years' events considerably better off. The cottager squatters went back to their normal lives, cutting peat on the bog, while Augustus sat in his new home, a monument to living in peace with one another, wondering what to do next in his life.

## Chapter 6

# AUGUSTUS ENDS HIS ASSOCIATION WITH MYNYDD BACH

AUGUSTUS BRACKENBURY ENDURED MUCH difficulty in pursuit of his quest to be a successful and well respected landowner on Mynydd Bach. However, by 1826, he had started to contemplate selling his estate, as the difficult events of that year unfolded. Those incidents made it hard for him to predict a viable future for himself on Mynydd Bach. After all, there was no point suffering ill feeling, just for the sake of it. Nonetheless, it wasn't until the following years, 1827-29, that Brackenbury actually drew up the plans and documents needed in order to sell his estate, in lots.

The Llanrhystud Myfenydd Enclosure Act encompassed 5,000 acres of waste land, spread over eight parishes in total, and Augustus had purchased 856 acres for the sum of £1,750. Brackenbury's estate was located in only three of these parishes: Llanrhystud, Llangwyryfon and Lledrod.

When he bought the estate, in 1819, he acquired it in seven lots (numbered 8, 10, 11, 12, 13, 14 and 15) of the actual Enclosure Act. The exact location of each lot is uncertain, and it is not known how much Augustus paid for each one, but the area of each lot is known. Lots 8, 10 and 11 encompassed 346 acres and were known as the *Gors* (translated 'bog', and an accurate description of the type of land that it was) and lots 12, 13, 14 and 15 were known as *Blaenau* (which could be translated as 'source', for it was the area where the three rivers Camddwr, Wyre and Beidiog started their course to the sea, or 'front' which is the Welsh translation for *blaen*). This second allocation amounted to 493 acres.

Most of *Gors* was in the parish of Llanrhystud, most of *Blaenau* in the parish of Lledrod. A portion of both areas was located in the parish of Llangwyryfon. There seemed to be little feasible means of going from one part of the estate to the other, other than a poor road between Troedfoel and Blaencamddwr.

During his time on Mynydd Bach, Brackenbury paid most of his attention to the *Gors* portion of his estate, where he built houses (of which three houses and two cottages managed to survive the wrath of the locals) and some fences and roads. Augustus spent a great deal of his money developing the *Gors*. He constructed a road between Troedfoel and Bwlch y Mynydd and it is still called *Lôn Sais* (Englishman's road), today. It is surprising that he expended most of his initial energy and money on this part of his estate, as the land here is of much poorer quality than that on the *Blaenau* portion.

The *Gors* was some 800 feet above sea level and it had some fruitful, dry land near Lôn Sais, but the quality of the land deteriorated as you approached the river Tryal. Next to this river were the peat fields, which were considered valuable in other ways. The *Gors*'s subsoil was of frozen clay that, over the centuries, had accumulated about six inches worth of good peat soil. Although good for claiming peat, it was unsuitable for grazing. This land was not drained properly, due to the topography, and rainwater would seep straight through into the clay. A wet summer posed a great deal of problems as the ground would be virtually impassable; if that were followed by a wet autumn and winter, it would be most unwise to put cattle anywhere near it. Sheep struggled, too, in the wet conditions, and they were prone to developing liver disease. However, mountain ponies seemed to adapt well to such terrain and managed to graze and move about quite comfortably.

The *Blaenau* part of his estate was some distance away from *Gors* and faced the settlement of Bronnant. This undulating land was partly dry and stony but there was also a flat, clayey portion, which was covered predominantly by rushes. Much of this land was suitable for sheep rearing. If Augustus had stayed on Mynydd Bach, he would have found it easier to make money here.

Why did Augustus decided to develop the more challenging end of his estate initially? It could be because this area is closer to the sea, about six to seven miles away from the shore, and closer to the two places where he would at times reside, Llanrhystud and Aberystwyth. He may also have thought to develop the most challenging area first, while he had plenty of funds to devote to the project. Somehow, one fears that he would not have been left alone to his ambitions, had he decided to build his houses on the *Blaenau* part of his estate, in those turbulent and difficult times.

Towards the tail end of the 1820s, Brackenbury realised that the likelihood of fulfilling his dreams on Mynydd Bach was low. He was certain, however, that he would leave his affairs in the area in order, and in the most profitable way for himself. He set about drawing up legal documents and plans for the dispersal of his estate to any interested parties. He ensured that his land was measured accurately and then drawn into a plan, and that a price was allocated to each piece of land. Most of these documents have, unfortunately, been lost, but six of them remain, including the following document for the sale of three acres from Lot 11, for the sum of £13, to the farmer Evan James, of Gryp, in the parish of Llanddeiniol. Considering that Brackenbury had paid around 2 guineas an acre for the land, but ten years previously, he seems, in this instance anyway, to have made a handsome profit on the sale of his estate. There follows an example of part of one of the documents concerning the sale of some of his land to Evan James, Gryp.

(Square brackets surround words which were in handwriting on the document)

> ARTICLES of an agreement made and entered into, the [eleventh] day of [March] 182[9] between Augustus Brackenbury, of Aberystwyth, in the County of Cardigan, for himself, his Heirs, Executors, and Administrators, of the one part, and [Evan James] of [Gryp] in the Parish of [Llanddinol] in the aforesaid

County [Farmer] for himself, his Heirs, Executors, and
Administrators, of the other part, as follows; viz.

THE said Augustus Brackenbury doth hereby agree
with the said [Evan James] to sell to him all that Piece
or Parcel of Land, being part and parcel of a certain
Allotment marked [11] in a Plan hereunto annexed, and
situate, lying, and being, in the Parish of [Llanrhystud
in the said County] bounded on the North [by a
Screed of land about three yards in breadth belonging
to the said Augustus Brackenbury and adjoining a
drain extending from West to East on the East by a
piece of land lately sold to David Phillips of Llyast-
y-conscience in the Parish of Llanrhystid aforesaid
on the South by a piece of land lately sold to David
Jones of Carreg Talwrn in the Parish of Llangwyryfon
in the said County and on the West by the lordship
of Haminiog] containing by Estimation [two] Acres
(more or less) [for the price of thirteen pounds]; and
that he, the said Augustus Brackenbury, will, at his own
expence, deduce a clear title to the said Piece or Parcel
of Land and Premises; and also that the said Augustus
Brackenbury, or his Heirs, shall and will, on or before
the [tenth] day of [July next] on receiving of and from
the said [Evan James] his Executors or Administrators,
the said sum of [thirteen pounds] for [the said two
acres (more or less)] so agreed upon as aforesaid, and at
the costs and charges of him the said [Evan James] his
Heirs, Executors, Administrators, or Assigns, execute a
proper conveyance for the conveying and assuring the
fee simple and inheritance of and in all the said Piece or
Parcel of Land and Premises, with their appurtenances
unto the said [Evan James] his Heirs or Assigns for
ever; and the said [Evan James] hereby agrees with the

said Augustus Brackenbury, that he, the said [Evan James] his Heirs, Executors, Administrators, or Assigns, shall and will, on the execution of such conveyance as aforesaid, pay the sum of [thirteen pounds] for the said [two] Acres [(more or less)] so agreed upon as aforesaid, unto the said Augustus Brackenbury, his Executors, or Administrators; and it is hereby further agreed by and between the said Augustus Brackenbury, and [Evan James] as follows; viz. … IN WITNESS whereof, we, the undersigned, have hereunto set out hands the day and year first above written.

> [Augs Brackenbury]
> [2 acres (more or less]
> 13 pounds amount of purchase money
> 13s / deposit
> Received the 19th day of March 1829
> the sum of twelve shillings
> Augs Brackenbury][7]

The land in the above document was turbary, a peat bog, which would have been the most valuable on his estate. The rest of his land would not have been priced so dearly. He started selling parts of his *Blaenau* estate as early as 1827, and one part was sold to David James, a cobbler of Bron-yr-helyg, Bronnant. He bought five and a half acres of dry grazing land from Lot 13 for £21, which still made a respectable profit of about £2 an acre for Augustus. Another local man, Daniel Davies, bought Cruglas, near Pantffynnon, on the *Blaenau* part of the estate, from Augustus for 3 guineas an acre in 1828.

By the time Brackenbury left Mynydd Bach at the

end of 1829, all of his land had been successfully sold off. Augustus had had noble intentions to create an estate of owner occupiers and tenants, a throwback, perhaps, to the old feudal estates. He had hoped to live comfortably in his castle, developing his estate for rearing animals and producing crops and, in turn, creating wealth for everyone involved. That was evidently not to be. On his departure, more cottager squatters seemed to be drawn to Mynydd Bach. When the Tithe Maps were published in 1843, a quarter of a square mile of Mynydd Bach was home to 40 cottages, with each one having an average of only 4 acres.

Brackenbury's decision to leave Mynydd Bach, just at the time when the locals had started to allow him to live in relative peace, is quite perplexing. There is no doubt that the toll of harassment and insecurity of the previous years had affected him greatly. However, it was not only the support of his neighbours on the hillside that he lacked on Mynydd Bach. It seems that the local gentry were unsympathetic, too, and their ambivalence towards his troubles was a disappointment to him.

It is quite obvious why the poor occupiers of the cottages dotted around Mynydd Bach would have been so affronted by the rich English gentleman from a faraway county. It is not as clear, why the gentry of Cardiganshire did not show greater friendship. It could easily have been due to his Englishness and the unfamiliar location (in terms of Wales) whence he originated that made the gentry unsure of him. No one knew much about his background or his family. Cardiganshire is a very parochial county, even today. It may also have been the case that Augustus simply wasn't good at socializing. He had already been described as odd by own his family in Lincolnshire; he possibly found it difficult to engage in friendships and felt far more at home dealing with and befriending people who were in his employment and who could, therefore, be expected to show him loyalty at all times. It may also be the case that, since his troubles on Mynydd Bach were so grave, he felt he didn't want to unload his worries onto comparative strangers, despite them being of similar birth and financial status to him. There is little doubt that that local gentry had no wish to associate with someone who was constantly so unfortunate in his local dealings. They probably, privately, sympathised a great deal with his plight. After all, as we have seen in Chapter 2, many of the local gentry themselves had been subject to the wrath of mobs and rioters, over the implementation of the Enclosure Acts, long before Augustus arrived on the Mynydd Bach. Brackenbury was once told by a magistrate that no Englishman would thrive on Mynydd Bach. In this instance, the magistrate's words were fitting. Augustus's inability to speak Welsh probably did him a great deal of harm, too, as did his lack of sensitivity in surrounding himself with imported workers from Shrewsbury.

Today, very little evidence of Augustus Brackenbury's time on Mynydd Bach remains. All the *tai unnos* built on the *Blaenau* part of the estate have completely disappeared, as have most on the *Gors* side of the estate. *Lôn Sais,* the road that the Englishman built to take him back to England, has survived.

★   ★   ★

There is no denying that Augustus Brackenbury possessed an entrepreneurial streak and would be willing to try anything once. It seems that he was quite adept at plunging into a project head first and, possibly, only thinking about any negative consequences much later. Two decades after leaving the hilly moor land of central Cardiganshire, he found himself at leisure in the city of London, hatching quite a different plan. It is not known for certain how he spent the two decades of the 1830s and 1840s, nor how many and what kind of businesses he was concerned with. But we do know, from C E Brackenbury's book, *The Brackenburys of Lincolnshire* (1983), that, towards the end of the 1840s, he was involved in the process of developing a patent for a new method of preparing common salt. He claimed that it would be far more economical than the current processes in place.

In 1849, he issued a circular, setting out the benefits of his new patent. He sought out investors who were willing to part with a mere £50 to develop a process that would see an annual return of £34,000. It all seemed far too good to be true and, like many other entrepreneurs in the salt market, his plan came to nothing.

The Greek classical poet Homer called salt a divine substance; the philosopher Plato thought that salt was especially dear to the Gods, and Emperor Augustus was not averse to giving it away for free to Romans, in order to procure favour from his people. Brackenbury felt that the substance which had built the Roman Empire would make him a fortune as well.

For centuries, in Britain and throughout the rest of the world, the old system of open-pan salt production had defied improvement. The system consisted of lighting a fire beneath a pan of brine, driving off the water in the form of vapour and collecting the salt crystals that formed and sank to the bottom of the pan. Primitive this system might have been, but, during the nineteenth century, most commentators in the salt industry regarded this process as not improvable.

This negative view failed to deter the thousands of entrepreneurs who hoped to change minds. Many patented new methods, and many within the industry did their level best to quash suggestions from anyone with a constructive idea.

Many of the salt proprietors saw no possible reason to welcome innovations. They enjoyed large profits from an old and wasteful process. The number of proprietors was small, and they were most suspicious of anyone wanting to join their ranks. Their monopoly made them intolerant of any competition. They were more than willing to join together, to crush a daring intruder.

It was in this trade, so full of envy, selfishness and malice, that Augustus decided to speculate, in the 1840s. Like most of the others who had entertained similar ideas, his made little headway in an industry ripe for change. It was, it seems, another plan that Brackenbury had hatched, which had gone somewhat awry.

Augustus had always shown a liking for the written word. He particularly enjoyed writing, and evidence of this can be seen in his lengthy letter written to the Home Secretary, Viscount Sidmouth in 1821, which is to be found at the National Archives in Kew. One could argue that he, like many of his other cousins, indulged in writing throughout his life. A few years before his death in 1871, he put some of his thoughts together and published a book in London; it was entitled *Aesop's New War Fables*. References to this book have been found in J F Kirk's *A Supplement to Allibone's critical dictionary of English Literature*, published in Philadelphia, in the United States, in two volumes, in 1891. However, the British Library has no record of this book, which may have been a 'vanity' publication, in that Augustus might well have published the book privately.

The title and text of Augustus's published work is of interest, in that it refers to war fables. He had himself been involved in incidents, which were known then and still are today, as 'The War of the little Englishman'. Augustus was evidently a keen student of battles and, no doubt, took a great deal of comfort from the thoughts and troubles of others on the topic.

It has been difficult to discover much further information about the life of Augustus Brackenbury, subsequent to his departure from Mynydd Bach. But the details surrounding his death are clearer. Augustus Brackenbury died, unmarried, on 11 August 1874, at the age of 82 years. At the time, he resided at 92 High Street, St John's Wood, Marylebone, London, where he was a lodger in the home of Eleanor Snowdon/Sawdon, who was a spinster of 70 years of age. Eleanor Snowdon/Sawdon had apparently been born at Scremby, and her occupation was recorded on the census returns of 1871 as being a 'Fancy Repository'. Augustus's death certificate states that the cause of death was *Senile Bronchitis*. A witness to his death was a certain A Smith of 35 Barrow Hill Road, Marylebone. The death certificate describes Augustus as a 'gentleman'. Brackenbury departed this life without writing a will, and no attempts were made to administer his possessions after his death. He seems, therefore, to have died a lonely old man.

Augustus Brackenbury had enjoyed a good innings, considering what must have been several stressful and turbulent periods in his life. He'd certainly lived life to the full and tried many a new thing, learnt some valuable lessons in Wales, and subsequently moved on to other enterprises and experiences. A frontiersman, he loved a new challenge and would put all of his efforts into succeeding. But failing didn't seem to dampen his spirits, either. It only made him more determined and stronger, to face the other mountains that he evidently wished to climb and conquer.

## Chapter 7

# BRACKENBURY'S MYNYDD BACH LEGACY

A SIGNIFICANT PROPORTION OF Mynydd Bach remains as common land to this day. The early nineteenth century hill dwellers angrily fought off attempts to have the area enclosed by the outsider and local man alike. This deep rooted right to have unrestricted access to the land has filtered down throughout the following two centuries. Local people have shown fierce loyalty, when subjected to threats over their freedom to the land. This allegiance has not been as apparent with regard to Welsh language issues, however. Many non Welsh-speaking outsiders now occupy Mynydd Bach homesteads. Little objection has been raised locally to this. In history, land has been much more important to the Mynydd Bach residents than the issues concerning the declining Welsh language.

Augustus Brackenbury, an outsider, tried unsuccessfully to enclose land on Mynydd Bach in the 1820s. Another example from the nineteenth century shows a local man, Isaac Jennings, incurring the wrath of the local inhabitants, much in the same vein as Augustus Brackenbury had done. Jennings spent £350 buying 95 acres of unenclosed land and twelve acres of Llyn Eiddwen from the Crown in 1847. Nearly a generation had passed since the departure of Augustus Brackenbury, but local opposition to the enclosure of land was just as strong. As soon as the walls to enclose his land had been built, by the following morning, he would find them reduced to rubble. Interestingly, Isaac Jennings was a respectable local man; he had established a Sunday school in one of his barns, and was a chapel leader. He was also a local Welshman, but the incidents over enclosing land showed that the mob would not respect those local men who looked for substantial advantage from the common land. This unsavoury episode put Isaac Jennings into an early grave at the age of forty-nine.

In the twentieth century, local opposition to any change in the *status quo* regarding the land has been as strong and vocal. At the end of the 1940s, many supported the Parish Council's reaction to the Forestry Commission's proposals to plant fir trees on vast swathes of Mynydd Bach. The root of the protest was that, once again, local people would be deprived of peat-cutting grounds. Much negotiation took place before the Commission was finally granted leave to plant trees, in the 1950s and 1960s, and this was to be on far fewer acres than were originally planned.

The events surrounding the compulsory purchase of land by the Forestry Commission may have inspired local poet B T Hopkins to write one of his best known poems. '*Ein Tir*' (Our Land) was composed in 1948, and in it Hopkins laments the loss of land, in varying forms, not only on the Mynydd Bach but also on many other hills in the surrounding area. Although he does not specifically mention losing land to English individuals in particular, B T Hopkins was certainly a nationalistic poet and a founding member of the Welsh National Party (*Plaid Cymru*) in the county, and he may have been one of the very few residents of Mynydd Bach publicly to voice opposition to the infiltration of Englishness into the area.

Disputes regarding the ownership of common land resumed in the 1970s, this time between the local Parish Council and a local farmer who owned the land surrounding Llyn Fanod. The farmer alleged that he owned the lake, but because much of the land in the Mynydd Bach area still remained as common land, many residents and the council took issue with his claim. After some legal wrangling, the farmer had to withdraw his claim, and Llyn Fanod remained part of the common land, with unconditional access being granted to everyone, to this day.

The 1970s saw very many outsiders, a good many of retirement age, successfully renovating homesteads which had fallen into virtual ruin on Mynydd Bach. No local opposition was shown to this predominantly English influx; indeed, it was welcomed by most because these newcomers were willing to invest money in the area and make the area more attractive to the eye. There were very few cases during this time of these incomers paying such high prices for housing that locals were compelled to look elsewhere to find an affordable home. In fact, in many cases, the perceived opinion was that many of these incomers were foolish in attempting to waste their efforts and money in renovating such dilapidated buildings. Services, such as shops and, to a lesser extent, the local primary schools were given a temporary reprieve. As a result, Mynydd Bach became much less parochial, as the proportion of Welsh to non Welsh changed. The young Welsh people decided to move out of the area because Mynydd Bach was too remote and isolated and there was little to engage them with regard to work and entertainment, and not as a result of being unable to find affordable housing.

The evidence shows that the protection of common land has been more important to the psyche of Mynydd Bach dwellers than the issue of non Welsh speakers infiltrating the area, and renovating ruined houses on the hills. Brackenbury's legacy reinforces the fact that these rare tracts of common land remain as important today as they were in the early nineteenth century.

## To conclude

The poet Jeremy Hooker wrote the following poem for radio in the late 1970s, during his time as an English lecturer at University College of Wales, Aberystwyth, and while he was living at Llangwyryfon, 'under' Mynydd Bach and not far from Lôn Sais.

### Englishman's Road

*First Voice*

Ruins among the rushes, stairs
mounting straight into the sky.
Walls that shelter sheep
from the west wind, or turn
like drystone streams, back
to their quarry source.
What is here but death?

*Second Voice*

Watch for the early settlers.
For the chamber-builders in stone,
who made a house for the dead.
For the shell–borne saint,
the houseless one, for whom
the universe is home.
Watch for an Irish or a Viking sail.
Watch for the castle-builders.
For incomers, early and late,
on the Englishman's road.

*First Voice*

What did they settle for,
the nightbuilders?
And why did he come,
the young man from Lincolnshire?
I should know why he came,
who also settle, and ask
with an English tongue:
what can I make of this
long-settled ground?

*Second Voice*

Take a long view from Mynydd Bach: let your eye rise and
fall with ridges that stone walls or bent thorns follow—
green dragon backs, crested like petrified breakers; yet
also the walls are always climbing or in flight. This is a
country of vast spaces: it rolls with hidden hollows to the
mountains of the north, against the sweep of sea –

> Preternatural grey,
> the mountains of Llŷn
> a chain of islands,
> or blue as spirit flame,
> or a lunula of beaten gold.

Here the buzzard with broad wings spread draws a widening circle, ringing an intricate pattern of commons and enclosures, whitewashed farms and red-roofed barns.

At night an irregular pattern of lights reflects the stars.

Here the western light is always changing, too quick for the eye though it notes

> Grey mystery
> of April, haunted
> by the curlew's salty cry,
> or August
> floating the hills,
> or Winter
> with a hard whiteness
> hammering the ground.

And what the light changes is only a face—face of a work vaster and more laboured than the pyramids; but continuing. For this is settled country, its pattern absorbent, deeply ingrained, but unfinished; without the finality of a coiled fossil, though it too is a life wrought in rock. And here these English words play on a surface through which they cannot shine, to illumine its heart; they can possess the essence of this place no more than the narrow road under the Welsh mountain can translate its name.

> Lon Sais it is called,
> not Englishman's Road.

Two hundred years ago
      the first nightbuilders came
and on these commons they built,
      invoking an ancient but unwritten right.
Then it was said:

*Squatter*
There shall not be any large farms or houses built on Mynydd Bach but they shall be pulled down, but if any poor man shall come, then we shall build a house and make a field and help him.

*First Voice*
Ruins among the rushes, stairs
mounting straight into the sky.
This too was the place of a skull.

*Second Voice*
Watch their craft by lanternlight.
It is late October. Now the night is not too short; strong winds and heavy rains are still to come. Their materials are all to hand. They have loaded on carts—

stone
timber
clods
soil
turf

Theirs is the hedge-bank craft. They pack the walls together with napes of mattocks. Turves cut from the moorland with a breast-plough cover the rafters; open coils of sheaves laid on the roof are fastened in place with reeds. The thatch covers from apex to eaves.

And now it is grey light, before the sun climbs on this mountain, as it seems to farmers on the richer lowlands, preparing to milk; and now with the first smoke, a soft plume on the roof, a man with a good arm takes his axe, and from the doorway hurls it. Where it falls he draws a line, rounding his portion of thin grass with rocky shoals.

It is settled. The long struggle with famine begins.

*First Voice*
Kite country. On the moorland
a car's wheelless corroding shell.
Slopes pitted with Iron Age graves
like stopped wells, and here,
green lanes leading—where?
Not a door to knock on; within
all's spiritless, a draughty space.
Ruins among rushes, stairs

mounting straight into the sky.
Walls that shelter sheep
from the west wind, or turn
like drystone streams, back
to their quarry source.
What can I make of this?
Emptiness. The exquisite, cruel
colours of decay. Death's absolute.

*Squatter*
Aye, it was dark, it was damp,
But we came homeless, and this
We held, for a time.
A huddle of hovels
If you like, and always
With enemies—
Where all's common it must be so—
Boyos from down below,
Fat-earth men, after their peat
And turf and grazing;
But worst, the weather, and this
Rockbacked, lock-jawed land.
But that man, that
Young sir, him we served, him
We gave what he could make
Of us. We half-roasted him.
And if at last we lost,
Still I tell you, this was no dream.
This was the Promised Land.
We were Bethel folk. We built

Stone on stone, a house of praise.
And what did He promise
But toil, sweat of the brow,
Bitter bread? So we laboured
And the spirit moved us, light
To the leaden hills, a feast
To the starving frame; laboured
I tell you, and praised, not
For honeyed ease, but at the last
Peace and an eternal rest.

*Second Voice*
And to this place, into this pattern,
          in the Spring of 1820, came
a small, dark Englishman
          from a hall in Lincolnshire.

It was not then Lon Sais
          where he rode on horseback,
curlews crying in the marshy fields,
          cuckoo calling back to cuckoo
until the mountain sounded hollow
          echoing their name.

Now the common land was his,
          for two guineas an acre,
but still it remained to settle:
          by building a house with a prospect,
          by improvement.

He called himself:

> Augustus Brackenbury,
> gentleman
> of the town of Aberystwyth
> in the county of Cardigan.

And the people of Mynydd Bach called him:

> Sais Bach.

It was not then Lon Sais,
        but truly, for a time,
the Englishman's road.

*First Voice*
Sais Bach, little Englishman:
why did he come?
Must I answer for him,
who make a shape of the place?

Which wilderness
does not know our image?
Where there is land and sea,
riches to claim,
a people without God, or with Him,
or gods of their own:
there is our image, and there
our rootless rongue.

    The stars
reflect our fires; we are mirrored
in histories we did not write.

    And here,
close to home, we have come
sword against sword, tongue
against tongue; and by our way
the people leave, and we pass them
       as if into our own.

*Second Voice*
And what the stranger comes to is darkness—not essentially
dark, but rather a light he cannot see by. For he brings
with him a mist, which is not the mist of these hills which
bears them away yet is part of them, and in its clear drops
globes their world; but the mist that swirls from his mouth
and clouds his eyes.

Behind the landscape he sees
       there is another.
He cannot hint at
       mountains and fields unseen,
deep and distinct in their native light.

These are measured heights. They are mapped and named;
but still, from without, essentially unknown. For here
these English words play on a surface through which they
cannot shine.

*First Voice*
I should know why he came,
who also settle, and ask
with an English tongue:
what can I make of this
long-settled ground?

*Augustus Brackenbury*
Here was a track like a dry river-bed
with cart ruts and stones.
So it had been all the way uphill
from Aberystwyth—where in all that country
I found tolerable company.
All around me was mountain wilderness,
with hovels on my ground
and dark, unsmiling faces. To these
I addressed myself kindly,
but in silence they stared back,
understanding not a word. Yet
this was a day when the sun shone
and cuckoos and curlews called
as if to greet me. And what I saw
was not a hostile wilderness
but a gentleman's seat, a fair prospect,
my estate, my establishment.
There, as in a landscape
of the English school, I saw
wild nature subdued to parkland
and the people graced with benevolence.
Here I would plant myself, and like

a spreading oak shelter my dependents.

*Second Voice*
How could he know where he was,
      or that on that mountain,
where he held himself proudly, he was
      a small, black speck crawling,
caught in the weave of a pattern
      into which he had blindly come?


How could he know where he was?
      Or others before and after him?
incomers, early and late,
      on the Englishman's road.
Castle-builders, makers
      with words or stone.


The ruins are taken back.
      From north to south,
the country echoes their names.

In the year of Waterloo
      enclosure surveyors came.
The women showed them a pit.
      Next time, they said,
bring a sack for your bones.

*First Voice*
Habitations of wretchedness,
      generality of the suffering poor.

*Squatter*
That was their truth, not ours,
Not the whole of it.
We were hungry for land;
Out thin grass kept a thin flesh
Firm: peat for our fires, oats,
A few sheep; for the rest,
Harvesting of corn and potatoes
In the seasons, or crawling
The narrow seams of Ystwyth,
Under the leaden hills.
But with spirit for that, so
Our common rights held, so
In smoke-filled darkness
Grace lit our spirit flame.
I tell you, this was no dream.

*Augustus Brackenbury*
I saw a promise in that land:
of Hafod and Thomas Johnes,
of a seat gracing the wilderness.
I saw a park watered by streams
of Mynydd Bach, prosperity
for all, a gentle culture, and a civil tongue.

*Squatter*
But that man, in his face
We saw a dream, his dream,
Ourselves its material.
Graciously he spoke,
A gentleman of fashion, or
After their fashion,
A gentleman. But I ask you,
What makes a man? Aye,
And what did he say?
Few understood, but I knew
His tongue and its meaning:
This is my country: be
Honoured that I come for you
To serve me, and improve you.
And what did we say?

There shall not be any large farms or houses built on
Mynydd Bach but they shall be pulled down.

*Second Voice*
There is law, and there are rights.
Those who claim rights need a strong hand to hold them.

Guineas may buy a man the law, but if he is far from his
kind, if between him and the law there comes an invisible
but immovable body, of language and loyalty, then he too
may hold his own, and pay for strong hands to grasp it.

Then the struggle is hand to hand.

*Squatter*

Was not John Jones son
Of David Jones shamefully
Abused, his horse and cart
Plunged in a bog?
Joshua Davies also—his cart
They broke, and stole his turf.
And Elizabeth Jones,
Going from service on a visit
To her parents, did not Brackenbury
And one of his bullies drag her,
With imprecations, to a deep moat
Surrounding his castle? Aye
And would have thrown her in,
Only one who heard her cries
Ran to help—and was threatened
With a musket to his head,
His lip gashed with a blow
From the muzzle. This was so,
I tell you: these things
In a manner most barbarous
Have been done. And other
Atrocities (too numerous
To mention), no person passing
But insulted, assaulted,
Pursued and shot at.
This on the Sabbath too,
By bullies with fire arms,
Shovels and other implements
Fit for evil purposes.

What justice for us? None.
But I tell you, such cruelties
We will not endure.

*Second Voice*
Now again there are lights on the mountain,
        not lanterns but torchflames:
in their ruddy glow, a slow dance—
        shadowy figures
treading with measured deliberations.

They are shawled, they look like women;
but some are men's faces the lights shine on.

Brands colour them a deep blood-red. They might have
risen from the Iron Age graves, here to enact an antique
ritual, treading the measure of an ancient law.

*Augustus Brackenbury*
My estate is situated in the midst of the most desperate
characters, who commit all kind of depredations with
impunity. The encroachers are so numerous and so
lawless, that they aid and assist each other to enclose the
waste lands and to keep possession thereof. This country
is now labouring under a dreadful and deplorable want of
morality.

*Second Voice*
It is rights they come for. There are:

> Jack Rhos goch
> Tom Ffospompren
> David Jones Lledrod
> Jack y Crydd

and others with a good arm to hurl a brand.

They have lit a fire on the mountain.

They circle in a shadowy outer darkness beyond the flames.
They have vanished.

*Augustus Brackenbury*
I have found the peasantry of this part deceitful, treacherous
and false swearers. This definition of their national character
is agreeable to the general opinion now entertained of
them.
Because I am an Englishman I am never to impeach or
discover any one who should commit any outrage on the
property I possess.

*Second Voice*
Now the flames show what they consume: a house,
burning. An empty house, for there through the darkness go
Brackenbury and his bodyguard, shivering, weaponless.

He is almost used to this. Though this is the first firing,
twice before he has built, and twice the pickaxe has
unhoused him.

Now a lowland farmer, looking up, might think a red
moon was rising, with burning horns; but there are few
who do not know, and few who have not sworn.

*First Voice*
They have vanished; they have made
their marks on the mountain's face,
which does not regard them;
where the kite may prey
undisturbed, and cloud shadows
seem the only spirits.
What is here, in a place
of sheep and ruins,
with no door to knock on,
under a vast empty sky
which the noise of war planes fills?

*Second Voice*
Watch for the early settlers.
For the chamber-builders in stone,
who made a house for the dead.
For the shell-borne saint,
the houseless one, for whom
the universe is home.
Watch for an Irish or a Viking sail.
Watch for the nightbuilders.
For incomers, early and late.

*First Voice*
Ruins among the rushes, stairs

mounting straight into the sky.
Walls that shelter sheep
from the west wind, or turn
like drystone streams, back
to their quarry source.
This too was the place of a skull.
What is here but death?

*Second Voice*
The nightbuilders have gone—
        South, over the mountain,
to coalface and furnace;
        others were absorbed here,
their hovels taken in by stronger walls.
        Original floor and hearth stones
form a pattern with the new—
        all from the mountain.

*First Voice*
I will not make them a song;
        they have their songs.
Nor will I make them an elegy.
        In this pattern they live:
ridges with walls climbing or in flight,
        hedgebanks squaring the fields,
in all the work wrought in rock
        they show their hands,
and there in Bethel,
        flame of spirit
        house of praise.

Where
  if not in the place of a skull
    will we find
      a vision of the Promised Land?

*Second Voice*
This is Lon Sais. Augustus Brackenbury, gentleman, has
taken the road to Marylebone. There in 1874 he and his
memories will die. But here the memory of Sais Bach will
haunt the houseless commons of Mynydd Bach.

*Augustus Brackenbury*
I was a pioneer.
I would improve the waste.
But these people I could make
nothing of.
                I would be
*a tree planted by the rivers*
*of water, that bringeth forth*
*fruit in his season.*
They answered: *the ungodly*
*are not so: but are like*
*the chaff which the wind*
*driveth away.*

*Hiraeth*, they say,
*hiraeth*, as if only they
know longing. Lord,
what days I have seen,
buried alive, looking east

with the eyes of my heart!
O to have been a seed
on the west wind, borne
back to Lincolnshire,
if only to grass a grave!
Still I stayed, for a time.
The right was mine, the law
no Welshman would enforce,
because I was English…

*Second Voice*
These are measured heights: a practice run for war planes.
Here curlews come in March, and on a telegraph pole,
with wires running east and west, a buzzard settles, like a
carved figurehead. This is Lon Sais, under the mountain.

There are ruins among rushes in the near fields. The castle
of Sais Bach is a square ditch, with only moor grass to
impede the wind.

There are no lights on the mountain unless the moon,
or the beams of a car, driving north through miles of
darkness. There, where carts loaded and turf descended.
This is settled country, an intricate pattern of farms and
smallholdings, with Bethel in a hollow. A work wrought
in rock, vaster and more laboured than the pyramids; but
unfinished. And here these English words play on a surface
through which they cannot shine, to illuminate its heart;
they can possess the essence of this place no more than the
narrow road under the Welsh mountain can translate its
name.

The place Augustus Brackenbury could not possess
      Sais Bach has entered:
            memory calls back to memory
               echoing his name.

Lon Sais goes on.
Englishman's Road has ended.

# REFERENCES

1. H.O. 40/16. folios 831–850

2. Davies, Alun Eirug. 'Enclosures in Cardiganshire, 1750-1850', Ceredigion, VIII (1976-79), p.116.

3. Lewis, W. J. 'A Disturbance on Llanrhystud Mountain', *Ceredigion*, IV (1960), pp.312-13.

4. Williams, David. ''Rhyfel y Sais Bach' An Enclosure Riot on Mynydd Bach', *Ceredigion*, II (1952), pp.49-50.

5. H.O. 40/16. folios 831–850

6. Jenkins, David. 'Rhyfel y Sais Bach', *Ceredigion*, I (1950-51), pp.199-200.

7. Phillips, Richard. 'Ychwaneg am 'Rhyfel y Sais Bach', 1820-29', *Ceredigion*, VI (1968), pp. 320, 322.

# Further reading

★ denotes Welsh text

Brackenbury, C. E. *The Brackenburys of Lincolnshire* (Lincoln: The Society for Lincolnshire History and Archaeology, 1983).

Davies, Alun Eirug. 'Enclosures in Cardiganshire, 1750-1850', *Ceredigion*, VIII (1976-79).

Jenkins, David. 'Rhyfel y Sais Bach', *Ceredigion*, I (1950-1).★

Jones, David. *Before Rebecca: Popular Protests in Wales 1793-1835* (London: Allen Lane, 1973).

Jones, David J. V. 'More light on 'Rhyfel y Sais Bach', *Ceredigion*, V (1964-67).

Jones, D. J. V. 'Distress and Discontent in Cardiganshire 1814-1819', *Ceredigion*, V (1964-67).

Leach, Terence R. and Pacey, Robert. *Lost Lincolnshire Country Houses Volume II* (Burgh le Marsh: Old Chapel Lane Books, 1992).

Lewis, W. J. 'A Disturbance on Llanrhystud Mountain', *Ceredigion*, IV (1960-63).

Phillips, Richard. 'Ychwaneg am 'Ryfel y Sais Bach', 1820-29', Ceredigion, VI (1968-71).★

Phillips, Richard. 'Amgau Tir ar Fynydd Bach', *Ceredigion*, VI (1968-71).★

Phillips, Richard. *Dyn a'i Wreiddiau* (Yr Awdur, 1975).★

Williams, David. ''Rhyfel y Sais Bach' An Enclosure Riot on Mynydd Bach', *Ceredigion*, II (1952).

*The War of the Little Englishman* is just one of a whole range of publications from Y Lolfa. For a full list of books currently in print, send now for your free copy of our new full-colour catalogue. Or simply surf into our website

## www.ylolfa.com

for secure on-line ordering.

TALYBONT CEREDIGION CYMRU SY24 5AP
*e-mail* ylolfa@ylolfa.com
*website* www.ylolfa.com
*phone* (01970) 832 304
*fax* 832 782